D1557642

Metaethics

Metaethics
An Introduction

Andrew Fisher

Routledge
Taylor & Francis Group

LONDON AND NEW YORK

For mum and dad, Janet and David

First published in 2011 by Acumen

Published 2014 by Routledge
2 Park Square, Milton Park, Abingdon, Oxon OX14 4RN
711 Third Avenue, New York, NY 10017, USA

Routledge is an imprint of the Taylor & Francis Group,
an informa business

© Andrew Fisher, 2011

Notices
Practitioners and researchers must always rely on their own experience
And knowledge in evaluating and using any information, methods,
compounds, or experiments described herein. In using such information
or methods they should be mindful of their own safety and the safety
of others, including parties for whom they have a professional
responsibility.

To the fullest extent of the law, neither the Publisher nor the authors,
contributors, or editors, assume any liability for any injury and/or
damage to persons or property as a matter of products liability,
negligence or otherwise, or from any use or operation of any methods,
products, instructions, or ideas contained in the material herein.

ISBN: 978-1-84465-257-0 (hardback)
ISBN: 978-1-84465-258-7 (paperback)

British Library Cataloguing-in-Publication Data
A catalogue record for this book is available from the British Library.

Typeset in Minion Pro.

Contents

Preface

This book is intended for anyone who is new to metaethics. It is a survey of some of the main developments in the field over the past hundred years. It evolved from teaching material I have been developing over the past eight years. I thank all those students who took my metaethics course and helped me reflect on the best way to present these issues.

While I was teaching it became clear that, although there are a number of excellent detailed books covering metaethics, for example Alexander Miller's *An Introduction to Contemporary Metaethics* (2003), what was needed was a simpler book that would act as a springboard into the subject. I toyed with the idea of "An Introduction to An Introduction to Contemporary Metaethics" – but only momentarily! This is that book and I hope it will be a gateway into further studies in metaethics.

I would like to thank certain friends who have read and commented on complete drafts of the book. Rosie Fisher's insightful comments were massively helpful. Janet Fisher made me think and rethink the process of writing and could spot an error at fifty paces. I thank you both for your indefatigable efforts.

I am lucky to work with excellent colleagues. Jonathan Tallant and Christopher Woodard read a complete draft and kept me on my philosophical toes throughout. A number of others read specific chapters and gave very helpful comments. Isabel Gois, Uri Leibowitz, Gregory Mason and Neil Sinclair, I thank you all.

I am particularly grateful to two anonymous reviewers for Acumen whose amazingly helpful and honest comments meant this book is far more accessible and readable than it was.

Finally I would like to thank Rosie, Elizabeth and Freya for putting up with me while writing and talking about "the book" for far too long; their happiness, patience and love supported me throughout.

Introduction

If you are not confused then you are not paying attention.

(Tom Peters)

CHAPTER AIMS

- To explain what metaethics is, and how it differs from normative and applied ethics.
- To outline two considerations when developing a metaethical position.
- To explain some key terms and common misunderstandings in metaethics.

Introduction

We *know* that when Nero used Christians as human candles he did something wrong. It seems *true* to us that the civil rights movement is a good thing. It is a *fact* that racism is wrong. If a culture thinks it right to torture children to death then they are mistaken.

But can we really have moral *knowledge*? What is it for a moral claim to be *true*? In what sense is it a *fact* that racism is wrong? How can something be right and wrong independently of what people think?

These are all metaethical questions and it is the aim of this book to give you the resources to start to answer them. But why are these questions classed as metaethical? What is metaethics anyway?

One useful way of answering this question is by contrasting metaethics with applied ethics and normative ethics. Consider an analogy that will illustrate the contrast: imagine ethics as football. We can equate different things associated with football with the different disciplines of ethics. There are the *players*, whom we can think of as *applied ethicists*. Applied ethicists are interested in moral questions regarding particular issues such as whether it is wrong to have an abortion, how to allocate limited hospital funds, whether hunting is wrong, whether we have an obligation to give money to charity, whether human cloning is wrong and so on. Then there is the *referee*, who helps interpret the rules that the players are following. The referee can be thought of as the *normative ethicist*. The normative ethicist is interested in questions regarding the underlying principles that guide the applied ethicist. For example, in working out what is right and wrong, should only the consequences matter? What sort of people should we become? How do we weigh moral considerations? Finally, there is the football *analyst or pundit*, who does not kick a ball or interpret the rules for the players but tries to understand and comment on what is going on *in the game* itself. This is like the *metaethicist*, who asks questions about the very practice of ethics, some of which we shall consider below.

Notice then that "meta" in metaethics is not about being "next to" or being "transformed" or "changing", as the prefix is sometimes used. Instead, it means to "stand back from", to "think about" or "sit apart from" ethics. For this reason philosophers call metaethics a "second-order" discipline. Think then of metaethics as taking a bird's-eye view on the practice of ethics: the metaethicist peers down as intently as possible and tries to make sense of what is going on.

In some sense then "meta*ethics*" is a fairly misleading name, since sometimes people think it is going to involve practical questions about how to live their lives. However, it is not.

Furthermore, even though metaethics is probably as old as philosophy itself it has only really gained a sense of identity since the publication of G. E. Moore's *Principia Ethica* in 1903. So our discussions arise from works written after this date, but although the book is relentlessly contemporary in its focus, the issues can more often than not be traced much further back in the history of thought.

The types of metaethical question

If metaethics is about trying to understand the practice of ethics, then we can start to explain it by thinking about the various parts of that practice. Looking at ethics we can see that it involves what people *say*: moral *language*. So one strand of metaethics considers what is going on when people talk moral talk. For example, what do people mean when they say something is "wrong"? What links moral language to the world? Can we define moral terms?

Obviously ethics also involves people, so metaethicists consider and analyse what's going on in peoples' minds. For example, when people make moral judgements are they expressing beliefs or expressing desires? What's the link between making moral judgements and motivation?

Finally, there are questions about what exists (ontology). Thus metaethicists ask questions about whether moral properties are real. What is it for something to be real? Could moral facts exist independently of people? Could moral properties be causal?

Metaethics, then, is the systematic analysis of:

(a) moral *language*;
(b) moral *psychology*;
(c) moral *ontology*.

This classification is rough and does not explicitly capture a number of issues that are often discussed in metaethics, such as truth and phenomenology. However, for our purposes we can think of such issues as falling under these broad headings.

Given (a)–(c), we can ask which, if any, should take priority in metaethics. Will thinking hard about language help us resolve issues regarding ontology and psychology? Will a clear understanding of ontology give us ways of answering questions in psychology and language? Or will thinking hard about psychology help us to better understand language and ontology? For example, if we conclude that there are moral facts (ontology) then this might suggest that when we make moral judgements we are expressing beliefs about those facts (psychology).

In metaethics the type of question that gets priority often echoes what was generally thought to be important in philosophy at the time. For example, Moore worked during a period when the central focus was on the philosophy of language. It is no surprise then that he starts with (a) and writes that the most important question in ethics is "How is 'good' to be *defined*?" (Moore [1903] 1993: 58). Yet later the philosophy of language and issues about meaning and analyticity became less important and this had a direct effect on metaethics. As Stephen Darwall *et al.* put it: "The narrowly language-oriented agenda of analytic metaethics was fully displaced … because of an uneasiness about the notions of 'meaning' or 'analytic truth'" (1992: 123).

So when studying the work of metaethicists it is worth asking whether (a), (b) or (c) has primary focus. Perhaps more importantly, one should ask which should take priority in metaethics, remembering of course that perhaps none of them should.

How should we develop a metaethical theory?

There is another fundamental methodological question that is well worth keeping at the front of the mind: what should the metaethicists be sensitive to when developing their theory? For example, if we are trying to answer questions about moral language – and, as philosophers, we take a particular approach to truth that differs from the view held by most people – then who wins? Do we go with the people on the street? Or the philosopher? This point can be best illustrated by revisiting our football example.

Imagine that the people in the crowd simultaneously shout "Penalty!" Leaving what the referee says to one side, imagine that the analyst or pundit thinks it clearly was *not* a penalty. She argues that despite the crowd's insistence, what they are saying is wrong. After all, she reasons, she has a vast amount of experience and has watched more games than most of them, she does not support either of the teams and therefore is not biased and she is in a much better position emotionally to understand what actually went on. What should we say in this situation? Was it a penalty or not? Do we take seriously the fact that 50,000 people simultaneously shouted the same thing at the same time?

So, when trying to work out the best analysis of moral practice, shall we start with how most people think and talk and try to build a theory around this? Or should we develop a theory and then either explain what people say in light of this or conclude that the way people think and talk is *not* a reliable guide to truth? If people think that certain moral claims are *always* true, does this mean that any metaethical theory should show this? Or rather, can the metaethicist claim to know more about these issues and agree that people are mistaken?

Of course, one might think it is a bit of both: that on some issues people's everyday thought and talk should direct our metaethical theorizing, whereas in other cases the philosopher should. But to take this route we shall need to tread carefully, for we need to give good reasons why on some issues great evidential weight is given to people and why in other cases it is not. As you read the rest of this book you will see metaethicists wrestling with this issue.

Why metaethics is a hard subject

Finally it is worth stressing that metaethics is a hard subject and that there are a number of reasons for this. The first is that it relies on, and varies with the developments in, other areas in philosophy. So, for example, if we say that moral *facts* exist then we'll need some ideas from *metaphysics* about the nature of facts and existence. Or if we think that we can only give synthetic definitions of moral terms then we'll need to be sensitive to issues in the philosophy of language regarding the analytic/synthetic distinction.

Consequently, in studying metaethics you should expect to spend time reading in other areas such as in metaphysics, philosophy of language, psychology, epistemology, phenomenology, philosophy of art, logic and so on. If you compartmentalize these subjects and believe you can study metaethics in isolation, it will be much tougher.

The second reason why metaethics is tough is its terminology. Metaethicists often introduce terms that are unfamiliar and peculiar to metaethics. For this reason I believe those starting to study the subject should make it a priority to get familiar with some basic terminology. The next section highlights key terms and the common misunderstandings about them. There is a glossary for reference at the end of the book.

Basic terminology and common misunderstandings

Moral realism

This is about what exists (ontology). The moral realist argues that moral properties exist and are in some way independent from people's judgements. For example, if moral realism is correct then we can say that the act of killing someone has the property of wrongness, and that it has it independently of whether people think it does.

Potential misunderstandings
- Moral realism is silent about the nature and origin of moral properties. So, for example, being a moral realist does not automatically mean that you are a theist. Moral properties can be natural or non-natural.
- Moral realists can hold that moral properties only exist because

people do. This is not the same as the claim that people can choose what is right and wrong (see Chapters 4 and 5).

- Just because the realists think that there are moral properties this does not mean they claim they know what things are right and wrong. It is perfectly consistent for the moral realist to claim that they have no better idea of what things are right and wrong than anyone else.
- Properties and facts are distinct, although the issues in this book (especially Chapters 4 and 5) do not depend on this distinction.

Moral non-realism

The moral non-realist argues that there are no moral properties or facts. Non-realism includes, among others, quasi-realism, anti-realism, error theory and irrealism.

Potential misunderstandings

- Even though the non-realist thinks there are no moral properties and facts, this does not mean they think there is no moral truth. This would only follow if they also held that a claim is true if and only if there are facts and/or properties that *make* claims true. But this is an independent claim about the nature of truth that the non-realist could reject (see Chapter 2).
- The non-realist can also be a cognitivist (see below).

Cognitivism

The cognitivist argues for two claims. The first is that when someone makes a moral claim they are expressing a belief. The second is that moral claims can be true or false; this is part of cognitivism because beliefs are the sort of thing that can be true or false. Philosophers call the potential for a claim to be true or false *truth-aptness*. Because beliefs are thought to be descriptions, cognitivism is sometimes called *descriptivism*.

Potential misunderstandings

- Cognitivism is not the view that moral claims are true, since it is quite coherent for the cognitivist to hold that all moral claims are false (see Chapter 3). This is a common mistake and it is best avoided by remembering that cognitivism is a view about truth-aptness and not about truth.

Non-cognitivism

The non-cognitivist argues that if a person makes a moral claim they are expressing a non-belief state such as an emotion: for example, to say that "killing is wrong" is to *express disapproval* towards killing. Put crudely, it is as if you are saying "Boo! Killing!" Consequently, because expressions of approval or disapproval are not the sort of things that can be true or false, the non-cognitivist thinks that moral claims are not truth-apt in the way that the cognitivist thinks moral claims are truth-apt.

Potential misunderstanding
- Non-cognitivism is not the view that moral claims are about our own mental states. For example, it is not the claim that "killing is wrong" really means "I disapprove of killing". In fact, this would be a form of cognitivism, which asserts that when we make a moral claim we are describing a mental state, in this case my disapproval of killing (see Chapter 2).

Naturalism and non-naturalism

The naturalist claims that the only things that exist are those things that would appear in the scientific picture of what exists. The non-naturalist thinks that there are some things that exist that could not show up on the scientific picture of what exists. So, for example, pleasure, salt and electrons would be natural things whereas God would not be (see Chapters 4 and 5).

Potential misunderstandings
- You could be a non-naturalist and deny that God exists. All you are committed to as a non-naturalist is that there are some things that exist that would not show up in the scientific account of what exists.
- You can be a naturalist but *not* be a moral realist because all that the naturalist is committed to is the claim that if moral properties exist then they would be natural. This leaves it open that there may be no moral properties. Equally, you could be a non-naturalist but

not be a moral realist, thinking perhaps that God exists but that he does not have anything to do with morality.

Internalism about motivation

The internalist about motivation thinks that when we make a moral judgement we are motivated as a matter of conceptual necessity to act in accordance with that judgement (see Chapter 8). So to judge that giving money to charity is right is necessarily to be motivated to give money to charity. For the internalist it is conceptually impossible that someone could be psychologically normal, make a judgement and yet remain unmotivated to follow it.

Potential misunderstandings
- Internalism does not entail that there is a necessary connection between judgement and action, since action is not the same as motivation. For example, someone could presumably be motivated to lose weight but never get around to doing anything about it.
- Internalism is not the view that true judgements motivate. It is simply the view that there is a necessary link between moral judgements (be they true or false) and motivation.
- The internalist does not hold that there is a necessary connection between judgement and reasons for action: there could be a necessary connection between judgement and reasons but not a necessary link between reasons and motivation.
- In metaethics the term "internalism" is also used to discuss internal reasons (see Chapters 7 and 8) and outside metaethics it is used to discuss mental content and epistemic justification.

Externalism about motivation

The externalist thinks that there is *no* necessary connection between making a moral judgement and being motivated. Moral judgements motivate an agent because of the agent's desires. For the externalist, then, the link between judgement and motivation is contingent on the psychological states of the agent.

Potential misunderstandings

- This is not the view that it is a matter of chance whether moral judgements will motivate. For example, it could be a psychological fact that most of the time most people have a desire to do the right thing and consequently most of the time most people are motivated by their moral judgements.
- In metaethics the term "externalism" is also used to discuss external reasons (Chapters 7 and 8) and outside metaethics it is used to discuss mental content and epistemic justification.

The layout of the book

Each chapter starts with a number of aims, and throughout each chapter I include summaries of key ideas and figures in metaethics.

At the end of each chapter is a list of key things to remember that can lead to confusion if forgotten. I finish each chapter with some suggestions for further reading.

At the end of the book I ask a number of questions that will help you to reflect on the issues discussed.

THINGS TO REMEMBER

- Metaethics does not prescribe how we ought to behave.
- Metaethics is a second-order discipline.
- Be ready to consult books discussing, for example, the philosophy of language, psychology, epistemology, the philosophy of mind and phenomenology.
- It is important to learn the terminology as quickly as possible.

Further reading

For some general surveys see Sayre-McCord (1986); McNaughton (1988); Darwall *et al.* (1992); Smith (1994: ch. 1); Jacobs (2002: ch. 1); A. Miller (2003: intro.); Shafer-Landau (2003); Fisher & Kirchin (2006: intro.); Schroeder (2010: ch. 1).

Particularly good for the methodology and taxonomy of metaethics is Timmons (1999: ch. 1). An excellent introduction to the philosophy of language is Miller (2007); metaphysics, Tallant (2011); epistemology, O'Brien (2006); psychology, Jacobs (2002); philosophy of mind, Lowe (2000).

1

The open question argument

The future historian of "thought and expression" in the twentieth century will no doubt record with some amusement the ingenious trick, which ... is the naturalistic fallacy.   (Frankena 1939: 464)

Why, then, isn't Moore's argument a mere period piece? However readily we now reject as antiquated his views in semantics and epistemology, it seems impossible to deny that Moore was on to something.
(Darwall *et al.* 1992: 116)

CHAPTER AIMS

- To introduce the open question argument (OQA) and how it relates to the naturalistic fallacy.
- To explain a number of problems with the OQA.
- To show how the OQA has shaped the metaethical landscape.

Introduction

Some things seem to resist definition. How might we define "person", "politics", "feminism", "beauty", "music", "yellow" or "society"? Being told that a person *is just* $H_{15750}N_{310}O_{6500}C_{2250}Ca_{63}P_{48}K_{15}S_{15}Na_{10}Cl_6Mg_3Fe_1$ or that music *is just* some combination of sound frequencies, leaves us unconvinced. Writing about how to define "yellow", G. E. Moore says:

> We may try to define it by describing its physical equivalent; we may state what kind of light-vibrations must stimulate the normal eye, in order that we may perceive it. But a moment's reflection is sufficient to [show] that those light-vibrations are not themselves what we *mean* by yellow.
>
> (Moore [1903] 1993: 62, emphasis added)

The question at the heart of this chapter is whether we think that "good" also resists definition. Do we feel short-changed, for example, if we are told that "good" is just "pleasure"? In *Principia Ethica* Moore argues that *any* proposed definition of "good" always leaves us feeling this way, and he takes this to be evidence that "good" is indefinable. Let us consider his argument.

G. E. Moore (1873–1958)

- 1925–1939: Professor of Philosophy at the University of Cambridge.
- Key text: *Principia Ethica* (1903).
- Argues that "good" is indefinable; that good is a simple, irreducible, non-natural, non-metaphysical property that is knowable through intuition. Using the OQA, argues that most philosophers had missed this and hence had committed the naturalistic fallacy. Metaethicists take him to be the father of contemporary metaethics.

Moore's open question argument

Consider how strange it would be for someone to agree that Prince Harry is a bachelor but then ask whether he is married; or for someone to agree that a chessboard has four right-angled equal sides but then ask if it is square; or whether the female fox with her head in the rubbish bin is a vixen. These are strange questions because once we understand the meaning of "bachelor", "square" or "vixen" then the answer is clear to us. Moore said of these types of questions: "the very meaning of the word decides it; no one can think otherwise except through confusion" ([1903] 1993: 72).

Moore calls these types of questions "closed". They contrast with what he calls "open questions", which are questions such as "Should a preacher vote Republican?", "Was Gandhi the greatest man who lived?" or "Is darts really a sport?" These are open because the meanings of "preacher", "greatest" and "darts" do not make the answers clear to us.

We can then make a general claim. If we can define "x" as "y" and if we understand "x" and "y", then if we ask whether a *particular* "x" is "y" the answer will be closed. If we *cannot* define "x" as "y", the question will be open.

Armed with this test, we can turn our attention to "good". We need to consider a definition of "good" and ask if a particular thing identified as "good" by the definition is in fact good. If such a question *is* "open" then arguably that definition is incorrect.

In *Principia Ethica* Moore puts forward his OQA: the argument that for any possible definition of "good" we can always generate open questions, which means that we cannot define "good".

Let us consider some examples. Think about the definition "good is pleasure". Now consider the question "Brad gets pleasure from gambling but is gambling good?" This certainly seems like an open question, since the answer is not obvious; understanding "good" and "pleasure" does not settle the matter. The question about whether gambling is good is fundamentally different in this respect from the question "Does that square have four sides?" If this is right, then we have evidence that we cannot define "good" as "pleasure".

Another definition of "good" might be "whatever makes the gods smile". According to Moore, if this is correct, then the question "Sacrificing sheep makes the gods smile, but is it good to sacrifice sheep?" will be closed. That is, if we know the meaning of "good", "sacrifice" and "the gods smiling" then the answer will be obviously yes. Yet it is not: such a question is open. It is fundamentally different from the question "Is Harry, the bachelor, unmarried?" In trying to answer the question about sheep and the gods, we would need to consider such things as animal suffering and the nature of God. Hence "good" cannot mean "whatever makes the gods smile".

Finally, let us consider an example that is perhaps closer to what some people actually think. Imagine if "Biologists discover the gene for goodness" were blazoned across the front of the magazine *New Scientist* (e.g. Cushman 2010). What would we think? If, for example, we are told that Bill is good, do we think it is obvious that he has this gene? Or if someone has been identified as having the gene, do we think that it is a closed question as to whether or not they are good? No: questions like these are open. Questions like these are fundamentally different from the question, "Snuffles is a female fox but is she a vixen?" It seems that "good" cannot be defined as having a particular gene.

Moore argues that we could carry on repeating this process for any proposed definition of "good". This leads him to conclude that "good" is indefinable.

> If I am asked "What is good?" my answer is that good is good, and that is the end of the matter. Or if I am asked "How is good

> to be defined?" my answer is that it cannot be defined, and that
> is all I have say about it.   (Moore [1903] 1993: 58)

He is not crossing his fingers and hoping that no one will ever come up with a correct definition of "good". Instead, he thinks we can know *a priori* that they will not. For Moore it is not simply difficult to define "good": it is impossible.

There is something else going on in Moore's discussion of "open" questions in *Principia Ethica*. He is not only interested in language and definition but also thinks that such talk of "openness" is relevant to ontological issues about properties. Specifically, Moore makes the claim that *because* "good" is indefinable the property good is irreducible. To see why he thinks this, it is necessary to consider the relationship between the OQA and what Moore calls the *"naturalistic fallacy"*.

Using the OQA to demonstrate the naturalistic fallacy

For the sake of argument, we shall grant Moore two claims: first, that the OQA shows that "good" means "good" and "good" alone; and second, that the meaning of a term is its referent – what it picks out. If these are combined then it is clear why Moore thinks the OQA has implications for the property of goodness, for if these claims are correct then "good" can only have one referent, and that referent cannot be anything but the property of goodness. For instance, good cannot be reduced to pleasure, well-being, happiness and so on. Good, in Moore's terminology, is a *simple quality*. Therefore Moore draws two conclusions in *Principia Ethica*: that "good" the term is indefinable and that good the property is irreducible.

Moore labels the mistake of thinking we *can* reduce good the "naturalistic fallacy". The name is not a particularly good one because the fallacy is committed if someone tries to reduce good to *any* property, whether it is natural or non-natural. For example, God is not a natural property but to claim that good is what God commands is still to commit the naturalistic fallacy. The key thing to remember is that if someone tries to reduce the property goodness, then they have committed the naturalistic fallacy.

Moore believed that by using the OQA he had shown that Mill, Kant, Spencer, Rousseau, Spinoza and Aristotle had all committed the naturalistic fallacy. This is quite some charge! If he can make it stick then he has cleared away some of the most influential thinkers in the history of ethical thought. However, most metaethicists think Moore's OQA has problems.

Problem 1: is the open question a trick?

Imagine that someone has arrived at a definition of "good" – perhaps "what we desire" – and consequently believes that "x is what we desire but is x good?" is a closed question. Furthermore, she thinks that anyone who denies this and who claims that the question is open does not fully understand the meaning of the word "good". In this case, the OQA seems to be no *argument* at all, but rather an *assertion* that her definition is wrong.

Thus when the proponent of the OQA claims that a definition of "good" leads to open questions they are simply *asserting* the falsity of that definition rather than *arguing* that the definition is false. They are betraying their lack of conceptual clarity and begging the question against those wanting to define "good". If this is right then Moore's OQA is no argument at all, and Frankena was right when he wrote that Moore has played an "ingenious trick" on us (1939: 464).

How might Moore respond to this challenge? Is there a way to show that the proponents of the OQA are not simply assuming the falsity of the definitions under consideration? Perhaps. Consider an example where we ask people on the streets "x is a shape with seven sides, but is it a heptagon?" If they found such questions open – that is, if they scratched their heads and said, "don't know", or "well, I suppose it could be" – then would this lead us to think that we had it wrong, and that a heptagon was not a seven-sided shape? No: in fact, the people we asked would probably insist that we should not take their responses seriously. We can imagine them saying things such as, "Don't worry about me; I've never been good at geometry." In the mathematical cases, then, we are happy to say that people could be confused if they find questions concerning mathematics "open".

Now consider the moral case. If we think that "good" *can* be defined as "what we desire" and, as in the mathematics case, we take our definition on the street and ask people whether the things they desire are good. The important question is this: what if they respond as they did in the mathematics case, scratching their heads and saying "Well, I don't know" or "I'll need to think about this as I'm not sure"?

Arguably, in this case our reactions would be different. If people have these reactions in the moral case then this seems *prima facie* reason for us to rethink the definition. When it comes to the meaning of *moral* terms it would seem that the popular view matters much more than in maths. So if people do find questions concerning a definition of "good" open then this is evidence that there is a problem with the definition. Admittedly, this is weaker than Moore's OQA. We now have a challenge rather than an argument against those who try to define "good". Yet even though this version is weaker than Moore intended, it does suggest that the OQA is not just an ingenious trick (this sort of response is developed by Snare [1975] and Ball [1991]).

Problem 2: the paradox of analysis

The paradox of analysis is often discussed in conjunction with the OQA, although it is initially hard to see the link between the two. To try to do this we shall consider the paradox on its own and a solution to it and only then will we consider how it relates to the OQA.

The paradox of analysis states that there are convincing reasons to think that conceptual analyses – the breaking down of concepts into their constitutive parts – can be informative and unobvious, but also convincing reasons to think that they cannot. What are these convincing reasons? Concerning the first claim, we typically think that engaging in conceptual analysis can tell us something new and unobvious: that the philosophers who tell us through conceptual analysis that "knowledge is true justified belief", "truth is correspondence to facts", "causation is constant conjunction" or "God is that than which no greater can be thought" have told us something informative and unobvious. Consequently conceptual analyses can be informative and unobvious.

However, there are convincing reasons to believe that conceptual analyses could *never* tell us anything new or interesting. Imagine we are going to analyse a concept. To stand any chance of doing this correctly we need to know the *meaning* of that concept, since we cannot possibly know if we are on the right track in our analysis if we do not. Indeed, if we do not know the meaning then a correct analysis would be no more than a lucky guess. But if we must *already* know the meaning of a concept before we can give a correct analysis of it, then a correct analysis of it is not going to reveal anything interesting or informative!

So, we seem to have a paradox. There are convincing reasons to think conceptual analyses are informative and unobvious. Yet there are convincing reasons to think that correct conceptual analyses cannot be informative and unobvious. Notice that this conclusion is broader than metaethics. If the paradox holds, then it would apply to *all* conceptual analyses, wherever we find them.

Luckily, the paradox of analysis is no paradox at all. For it is possible to give correct conceptual analyses and reveal something informative and unobvious by doing so. There are a number of ways of showing how. The most widely accepted starts by noticing that "knowledge" can mean knowing *how* to do something. For example, we may know how to speak grammatically, know how to ride a bike and how to lunge in fencing. However, this could simply mean that we have the *ability* to speak, to ride a bike and to fence. Importantly, it does not follow that just because we have such skills that we could explain exactly what is going on in each activity. We could not list the rules of grammar or explain the physics of balance or the physiology of twitch fibres and so forth. Nevertheless, we still know how to speak, ride and fence.

This is relevant to the paradox of analysis because being sensitive to the possibility that "knowledge" can mean "knowledge how" allows us both to agree that we must know what a concept means before we can correctly analyse it and to claim this can simply mean we must know how to use the concept correctly. We could be just as unable to articulate what a concept means, as we are to explain the rules of grammar, the physics of cycling or the physiology of fencing. If this is true, then if someone did list what a concept means then this could be a revelation to us, teaching us something new and informative: just as we would learn something if someone explained why we stayed on a bike when riding, or what rules we were adhering to when talking, or how we gauged distance when lunging. Hence if knowledge can be about having certain abilities then an analysis of a concept can be interesting and informative and the paradox of analysis is no paradox at all.

We are now in a position to see why this is relevant to the OQA. If the paradox is not a paradox then the OQA fails, because – as we have just seen – true conceptual analysis can tell us something informative and unobvious. This means that, for example, it could both be true that we can define "good" as "pleasure" and true that arriving at this taught us something informative and unobvious. This in turn would mean that if we asked "Is *x*, which gives us pleasure, good?" the answer may not be obvious, even if we knew the meaning of "good" and "pleasure". Questions concerning the definition would be "open". But if that is right then we have shown the possibility of true conceptual analyses that give rise to open questions, something Moore's OQA cannot allow for. Therefore, our response to the paradox of analysis using the notion of know-how, has shown that the paradox is no paradox and that Moore's OQA fails.

Problem 3: not all true definitions need to be true by definition

The two problems we have considered so far allowed Moore the claim that if a definition is correct then this is decided by the *meaning* of the terms involved. In the above section we considered some definitions that were true and showed that they generated closed questions: it is a closed question whether Harry the bachelor is unmarried, the female fox in the garden is a vixen or the square chessboard has four equal sides. This then led to the generic claim that if we *can* define "*x*" as "*y*" and we *understand* "*x*" and "*y*", then if we ask whether a *particular x* is *y* the answer will be obviously yes; the question whether a *particular x* is *y* will be "closed". As Moore put it, when considering whether such a definition is correct, the "very meaning of the terms decide it" ([1903] 1993: 72).

So, if it turned out that there could be a correct definition but the meaning of the terms did not decide it, then it could be the case that "*x*" *can* be defined as "*y*", and we understand "*x*" and "*y*", yet questions about whether a particular *x* is *y* would be *open*. In other words, such a definition would be immune from the OQA. This is precisely the problem that will be considered in this section. In essence, it says we have good reasons to resist the idea that a true definition is one that is true in virtue of the meaning of the terms involved.

This problem for the OQA starts from the observation that there *are* true definitions that are *not* true in virtue of the *meanings* of the terms involved. For example, consider the theoretical definition "water is H_2O". Is this definition true? Yes. Does the meaning of the terms "water" and "H_2O", decide the matter? No. That is to say, if the definition is true and water *is* H_2O then we come to know this by empirical investigation in the laboratory, rather than by conceptual analysis in the classroom. The scientist does not engage in trying to establish the *meaning* of terms through conceptual analysis but rather investigates what the world is actually like. This in turn means that it is *open* to ask "Is *x*, which is H_2O, water?" It is open because it is possible that the scientific community has it wrong. Consequently, there are at least some definitions, theoretical ones, which are immune to the OQA.

If we want to defend the claim that good is, say, pleasure, then it would be great if we could show that this is like the claim that water is H_2O. If we could do this then our position would be immune to the OQA. To do so, though, we would need to establish that we had the right to claim such a similarity. For example, we might try to show that we can use empirical evidence to establish that "good" picks out some natural property, or show that we use "good" to intend to refer to *causal* properties that are responsible for what we think of as relevant to goodness. If this sort of move were possible then definitions of moral terms would be immune to the OQA. In Chapter 4 we take a look at Cornell realism, which takes on precisely this task.

There are a number of other problems for Moore's OQA. However, rather than discussing these we shall consider why it is that even though metaethicists typically reject Moore's argument, "it seems impossible to deny that Moore was on to something" (Darwall *et al.* 1992: 116). In the next section, we shall consider one reason why this might be the case.

Can we really define "good"?

Thus far, we have looked at some of the many problems for Moore's formulation of the OQA. Arguably, rather than showing why we cannot define "good" it assumes we cannot, relies on an incorrect notion of analysis and depends on the false claim that all true definitions are true in virtue of the meaning of the terms involved. However, even though Moore's own version of the OQA seems problematic, many philosophers think he might have been on to something.

To understand this, we should ask whether we could find a common definition of "good" that would capture what people mean when they say, for example, "it's good to help the homeless" or "it's good to keep promises" or "it's good that Saddam Hussein was executed". It might be tempting to answer that it could be possible by constructing a massive collection of everything desirable in a definition. Such a definition might run: "good is what gives us pleasure *and* what we desire *and* what God says *and* what makes us happy *and* what helps society and so on".

But the possibility for such a response is bleak. If this approach is tempting then when, for example, the famous atheist Richard Dawkins says "keeping promises is good" this would *mean* "keeping promises gives us pleasure and is what we desire and is *what God says* and is what makes us happy and is what helps society and so on". Can this be right? Is it really true that when people use the term "good" they really *mean* such a massive set of things?

Furthermore, to make the question "Is 'good' definable?" clearer, notice that answering no is not the same as saying we cannot identify things as good. We may in fact be great at picking out all those things that are good, but still hold that we cannot define "good", for there is no reason to suspect that the only way we could identify good is via holding a definition. After all, the same is not true of other things. Coming to realize we love someone does not require that we have a definition of "love"; if it did people would feel a whole lot lonelier. Therefore, we can still be morally good and be able to recognize what is good, even though we cannot define "good". So again, can we define "good"?

I suggest if we take a note of the past few paragraphs and consider the question then the answer most people would give is no. We think good somehow outstrips any possible definition; good seems different, loftier, more important and more significant in a way that a definition would fail to capture. Being told that, for example, "good" just means "pleasure" seems to miss something fundamental to good. Of course, this is imprecise, so can we make any more of these basic thoughts? And if we can, then how might this relate to the OQA?

Following a suggestion from Darwall *et al.* (1992), we should note is that the OQA needs a more modest ambition. If it sets itself up as a knock-down argument, then it is bound to fail. Instead, we should think of it as a challenge. As we mentioned above, it is a way of forcing those who define "good" to *explain* why we find questions generated from their proposed definitions open.

Once we allow this then it seems that the plausibility of the OQA will depend on how we might explain why people find questions open. Therefore, if we want to defend the OQA we need to ask what explanation we could give. Here is a suggestion similar to one made by Darwall *et al.* (1992).

Claiming that something is "good" *moves* us. For example, claiming that it is good to keep our promise means we shall have (at least some) motivation to do so. It would be very odd for someone to say, "It is good for me to keep my promise, but what has that to do with me?" Moral judgements – in virtue of being moral judgements – seem to motivate those people who make them (for more on this, see Chapter 8). This observation, then, may give us one way of explaining why people find questions concerning proposed definitions of "good" open: for we might think that if we try to define "good" the definition will not preserve this practicality.

For example, imagine we take "good" to mean "pleasure". Now, if we judge that something is pleasurable this could, of course, move us but it may not; it could leave us completely cold. It does not sound odd to say, "Driving at high speed would be pleasurable, but what has that got to do with whether I speed or not?" Whereas it *did* sound odd to say "It's good, but what's that got to do with me?" But if "good" just means "pleasure" then arguably we should not get such a variation in our reactions to these statements.

The suggestion to support the OQA, then, is that we find questions concerning definitions of "good" open because when we make a judgement that something is "good", this will always motivate us. This is only a challenge, because at some point a definition may be given that *could* capture such practicality, but minimally what this version of the OQA does is to force a response from those who try to define moral terms. It is like saying to them, "*Show us how your definition can capture the practical nature of morality*". However, to finish this chapter we shall consider the wider influence of the OQA.

Conclusion and influence

We can reject *Moore's* version of the OQA for the three reasons stated above: it begs the question, relies on an incorrect notion of analysis and depends on the false claim that all true definitions are true in virtue of the meaning of the terms involved. Yet it would be unwise to confine it to the history books. The OQA has had, and continues to have, a considerable influence.

We suggested that the OQA is most successful when thought of as a challenge to those who attempt to define "good". Can they explain why most people find questions generated from their proposed definitions open? One reason we gave is that definitions of "good" fail to capture the practical nature of judgements about what is good. It is this practical feature of morality, arguably highlighted by the OQA, which led to the dominance of non-cognitivism in the immediate period succeeding *Principia Ethica*.

To see why, first consider cognitivism. This is the view that when we make a judgement – whether that is about the weather, the time, the fastest bird of prey or the local fish and chip shop – we are expressing a belief. So, for the moral cognitivist, when I say "It is good that some drug companies freely distribute retroviral medication", I am expressing a belief about the goodness of this action.

The problem is that beliefs do not seem to be essentially practical but rather inert. I can have a whole host of beliefs about a whole host of things and be singularly unmoved. But if this is the case, and if moral judgements are expressions of beliefs, then we ought to be able to say, "It is good to give to charity, but what has that got to do with me?" However, as discussed in the previous section, this kind of claim seems strange because moral judgements do seem essentially to be practical. The *cognitivist* then has a problem. If they are right and moral judgements express beliefs but beliefs are not essentially practical, moral judgements cannot be essentially practical. Yet moral judgements seem to be necessarily linked to motivation and hence cognitivism appears to be mistaken.

This contrasts with what the non-cognitivists say. They seem to be able to capture the practical nature of moral judgements. For if non-cognitivism is right, then moral judgements are expressions of *non-belief* states such as desires; and importantly, desires are precisely the sort of mental state that *can* move us. If I am thirsty and desire a drink then this is likely to get me off my seat to flick the kettle on; if I desire to go to sleep I am likely to go to bed; if I desire to cycle then I shall get my bicycle out. The point is that desires move us and if moral judgements express our desires then moral judgements *can* capture the essentially practical nature of morality. Non-cognitivism has been the biggest benefactor from the OQA because the OQA suggests that morality is essentially practical; it seems that the cognitivist cannot capture this practicality whereas the non-cognitivist can.

However, if moral judgements express non-belief states such as desires, then this may bring its own problems, for it seems to suggest that morality is somehow similar to matters of taste and we may think that moral considerations are weightier than this. Furthermore, if moral judgements express desires, we might be concerned with how we can talk of *truth, convergence, progress, disagreement* or *logical inference*, all of which are features of moral talk. In the next chapter, we shall take a closer look at one non-cognitivist theory called *emotivism*, and ask how well it fares.

THINGS TO REMEMBER

- The OQA and the naturalistic fallacy are different things.
- The naturalistic fallacy refers to *any* attempt to reduce moral properties – including those that attempt to reduce them to *non-natural* properties.
- Discussions related to language and discussions related to properties are distinct from one another.
- Moore *does* think we *can* make judgements about what *is* good. For example, we could say that it is good to love your neighbour. What Moore argues against is the ability to say what "good" would mean in such a judgement.

Further reading

Moore's views are outlined in Moore ([1903] 1993: ch. 1) and Schilpp (1952). A good commenty on Moore's philosophy is in Baldwin (1990). Miller (2003: ch. 2) gives an excellent overview of Moore's OQA and the surrounding controversies. Darwall *et al.* (1992: §1) gives a suggested defence of the OQA. Frankena (1939) is a classic criticism of the naturalistic fallacy. Two hard papers that look at the linguistic side of the OQA are Snare (1975) and Ball (1991). Two other hard papers that discuss the OQA in relation to synthetic definitions are Horgan & Timmons (1992) and Rosati (1995). Other postive discussions of the OQA include Altman (2004) and Strandberg (2004). For a nice short discussion of the paradox of analysis see Clark (2002).

2

Emotivism

If we take in our hand any volume; of divinity or school metaphysics, for instance; let us ask, Does it contain any abstract reasoning concerning quantity or number? No. Does it contain any experimental reasoning concerning matter of fact and existence? No. Commit it then to the flames: for it can contain nothing but sophistry and illusion.   (Hume [1748] 1995: 165)

Under the pretence of ultimate wisdom [Ayer's book] guillotines religion, ethics and aesthetics, self, persons, free will, responsibility and everything worth while. I thank Mr Ayer for having shown us how modern philosophers can fiddle and play tricks while the world burns.   (D'Arcy, quoted in Stevenson 1944: 265)

CHAPTER AIMS

- To outline cognitivism and non-cognitivism.
- To explain why Ayer rejects cognitivism and adopts non-cognitivism.
- To state the main motivations for emotivism.
- To show how emotivism raises issues about relativity, truth and normativity.

Introduction

Morality keeps us awake at night and our moral compass guides us to think things we do not want to think and to do things we do not want to do; where morality is concerned we shout at the television, we form and break relationships, make career decisions, weep and laugh. Morality affects us in a deep and sometimes dramatic way. Emotivists argue that they are in a better position to capture this feature of morality than rival theorists are and that they can better capture the practicality of moral judgements that we mentioned in the previous chapter. This is because for them to make a moral claim is to express an emotion and emotions, they argue, can move us in these deep and dramatic ways.

Yet even though emotions appear to capture the dynamic nature of morality, they do not seem to fit well with other features. For example, emotions cannot be true or false, whereas it seems that moral claims can. Emotions seem beyond rational criticism, but our moral beliefs do not. Emotions do not seem objective or to have authority over us in the way we'd expect right, wrong, good and bad to have. In this chapter, we shall consider one emotivist position and ask whether it can respond to these sorts of worries.

A. J. Ayer (1910–1989)

- 1958–1978: Wykeham Professor of Logic at the University of Oxford.
- Key text: *Language, Truth and Logic* (1936).
- Defends emotivism, the view that when we make a moral judgement we are expressing an emotion rather than just describing something. For Ayer moral judgements cannot be true or false, and there can be no genuine moral disagreement.

Ayer's verification principle: a way of separating sense from nonsense

Ayer is a "radical empiricist". He believes that philosophy is the hand-maiden of science and that the only world there is, is the one that is dealt with by science. For him, philosophy is a second-order discipline whose job is to refine and analyse the methods of science and argumentation. As part of this empiricist outlook, Ayer was committed to the principle of verification, the claim that a statement is meaningful if and only if we can in principle empirically verify it or if it is analytically true. Consider two statements:

(a) There will be a measles pandemic in the year 2050.

Even though it is not 2050, we know that *if* in 2050 a large group of people contract measles across a wide geographical location then this would *empirically verify* (a). Thus by using Ayer's verification principle we can show that (a) is meaningful. Consider another example:

(b) All brothers are male.

This is not empirically verifiable but it is not meaningless because it expresses an analytic truth. That is, once we know the *meaning* of the terms involved, we recognize (b) as true. Thus by using Ayer's verification principle we can show that (b) is meaningful.

This, then, is Ayer's verification principle. If we accept it we have a powerful way of sorting meaningful from meaningless statements. We should consider a statement and ask whether it is empirically verifiable or analytically true. If it is neither then it is meaningless.

In *Language, Truth and Logic* Ayer applies this principle to the traditional subjects dealt with by philosophers. His conclusions are radical. For instance, of metaphysics, he writes, "The metaphysician ... does not intend to write *nonsense*. He lapses into it" ([1936] 1974: 60, emphasis added), and of religion, "Our view [is] that all utterances about the nature of God are *nonsensical*" ([1936] 1974: 153, emphasis added). So Ayer claims that when, for example, the theologian talks about "God's transcendence" or the metaphysician talks about "Forms and particulars" they are talking nonsense. This is because claims about God's transcendence and claims about Forms and particulars are not empirically verifiable. This is not to claim that statements in theology and metaphysics are false; rather, if Ayer is right, they are meaningless, equivalent to statements such as "bathrobe tall llama on the barbeque" – total babble, and worse than false!

What happens when we apply the verification principle to ethics? Ayer claims that "sentences which simply express moral judgements ... are *unverifiable*" ([1936] 1974: 144, emphasis added). Thus, given that Ayer does not think statements about ethics are analytic, we would expect him to claim that they are meaningless and that they are in the same category as statements made by the theologian or the metaphysician. Surprisingly he does not say this, since he believes moral claims *are* meaningful. We shall return to this apparent anomaly below. However, our first task will be to show how the verification test plays its part in the development of Ayer's overall metaethical view.

Ayer's rejection of cognitivism using the OQA and the verification principle

For the sake of argument, Ayer grants the truth of cognitivism: the view that when we make a moral judgement we are expressing beliefs that describe the world. For example, when I judge that it is good to give money to charity, I am describing charity as having the property of being good. He then asks what this might mean. What are the moral properties that we are describing? Ayer claims there are only two options:

(a) We are describing something *natural*.

According to (a), to judge that something is good, bad, right, wrong and so on is to judge that it has some natural feature, and by "natural" philosophers mean something like "the subject matter of the natural sciences and also of psychology" (Moore [1903] 1993: 92). So, for example, judging that giving money to charity is good might be the same as judging that giving money to charity gives people pleasure. Ayer calls (a) *naturalism* and rejects it using the OQA. He writes:

> [S]ince it is not *self-contradictory* to say that some pleasant things are not good … [e.g. taking heroin] it cannot be the case that the sentence "*x* is good" is equivalent to the sentence "*x* is pleasant" … And since it is not self-contradictory to say that some pleasant things are not good, or that some bad things are desired, it cannot be the case that the sentence "*z* is good" is equivalent to "*x* is pleasant", or to "*x* is desired".
>
> ([1936] 1976: 139, emphasis added)

Ayer thinks the OQA can show that any proposed naturalistic definition of ethical terms will fail and consequently that naturalism fails. Therefore, when we are making moral judgements we are *not* describing something natural. What, then, are we describing? Ayer thinks the only other option is that:

(b) We are describing something *non-natural*.

But Ayer also rejects (b), the claim that we are describing something which is *not* the subject matter of natural sciences or psychology. He thinks that to claim that something is non-natural is to claim that it is beyond empirical verification. However, as we have seen, Ayer thinks it is meaningless to talk about something beyond empirical verification. This means that (b) is false and that when we make moral claims we cannot be talking about something non-natural.

To sum up: Ayer believes that if we are cognitivists we face a dilemma. We must be naturalists (a) or non-naturalists (b). Both options fail. The first generates questions that should be closed but turn out to be open. The second fails because of the verification principle. Ayer argues that this all shows that we should adopt *non-cognitivism* and that we should not have accepted cognitivism in the first place.

Ayer's non-cognitivism: aka emotivism

By rejecting cognitivism Ayer has to adopt *non-cognitivism*: the view that when we make moral judgements we are expressing a non-cognitive state. What are non-cognitive states? This is a good question made more difficult by the fact that the boundary between cognitive and non-cognitive states is vague. It is not obvious that we could give necessary or sufficient conditions for a mental state being one or the other. What is clear though is that in so far as the distinction is useful, emotions are non-cognitive and beliefs are cognitive. (We shall stick with this for now and return to it in Chapter 10.)

Ayer suggests that moral language operates differently from how it does in everyday non-moral judgements, despite apparent similarities. For example, because "is hot", "is wet" and "is dirty" are in the predicate position when we say "the plate is hot", "the grass is wet", "the bike is dirty", we think they are adding some factual content to our claims about the world. It seems as though we are describing the world – the plate, grass and bike – as having certain features. Yet regarding *moral* claims, Ayer writes: "The presence of an ethical symbol in a proposition *adds nothing to its factual content*. Thus if I say to someone, 'You acted wrongly in stealing that money,' I am not stating anything more than if I had simply said, 'You stole that money.'" (*ibid.*: 142, emphasis added).

If Ayer is right then when we use ethical predicates we make no claim *about* the world. For example, "killing *is wrong*", "stealing *is wrong*", "giving money to charity *is right*", "debt relief for developing countries *is good*" do not describe killing, stealing, giving money to charity or debt relief, as having certain features. So when we make such claims what are we doing? Ayer's answer is that we are expressing an emotion:

> If I say to someone "You acted wrongly in stealing that money",
> I am not stating anything more than if I had simply said, "You

stole that money". In adding that this action is wrong I am not making any further statement about it. It is as if I had said, "You stole that money", in a *peculiar tone of horror*.

(*Ibid.*: 142, emphasis added)

So when we state that "Bill acted wrongly by stealing that money", Ayer says we are expressing an emotion about Bill and not making a factual claim. Hence his position is called *emotivism*.

What is fundamental to understand is that Ayer is *not* saying that moral judgements describe our emotions. For example, Ayer is *not* saying that "killing is wrong" *means* "I get angry at killing". If he were saying this then he would be a cognitivist. That is, he would be claiming that moral judgements express beliefs about the world, in this instance about me being angry. Instead, he thinks that when we make moral judgements we are not *describing* anything; rather, we are *expressing emotions*. For example, when I judge that "killing is wrong" I am expressing my anger at killing.

The key distinction to keep in mind is that between expressing – what emotivists think we do when we make a moral judgement, and reporting – what cognitivists think we do when we make a moral judgement. This distinction becomes particularly crucial when we discuss emotivism and relativism below. Notice that everyone accepts that there are some expressive uses of language, for example, shouting "Ow!" when stubbing our toe. The point is that emotivists argue that moral language should be understood in this way as well.

Moral truth and moral disagreement

For Ayer there is neither moral truth nor moral disagreement. We shall take these in turn. If making a moral judgement is expressing an emotion, then a moral judgement cannot be true or false. Think about an expression of an emotion, such as anger. If a bus knocks someone off her bicycle and she expresses anger, we can ask whether she was really angry, but it makes little sense to ask whether the anger *itself* was true or false. This is because emotions do not *describe* the world as being a certain way and hence cannot describe the world accurately or inaccurately. Therefore Ayer believes that moral judgements are not truth-apt, since they express emotions, which can neither be true nor false.

As he writes:

> If a sentence makes no statement at all, there is obviously no sense in asking whether what it says is true or false. And we have seen that sentences which simply express moral judgements do not say anything. They are pure expressions of feeling and as such do not come under the category of truth and falsehood. (*Ibid.*: 144)

Concerning disagreement, Ayer thinks there are no genuine *moral* disagreements because when we make a moral claim we aren't making a claim *about* anything, so those claims cannot lead to a disagreement *about* what the moral world is like. Ayer would argue that it is a clash of emotions if I believe that capital punishment is wrong and you believe that it is right; I am expressing disapproval towards capital punishment and you are expressing approval towards capital punishment. So it is a mistake to believe there is *genuine moral* disagreement. But people *do* seem to be involved in long and heated discussions about moral issues, so what is going on? Ayer thinks that "we find, if we consider the matter closely [of supposed moral disagreement] … the dispute is not really about a question of value, but about a *question of fact*" (*ibid.*: 146, emphasis added). So all supposed moral disagreement is actually disagreement about non-moral issues.

To illustrate, imagine that Charlton Heston and Michael Moore are engaged in a heated debate about whether it is morally acceptable to own a gun. This certainly might look like a genuine moral disagreement. However, for Ayer what they are disagreeing about is not moral facts but non-moral facts. For instance, perhaps Moore thinks that handgun ownership leads to greater crime rates, whereas Heston disagrees. Or perhaps Heston thinks that increased gun ownership is good for the economy, whereas Moore disagrees. Of course, this explanation of why moral disagreements are not genuine does not mean that the disagreement will be any less heated, protracted or dramatic. It is just that if Ayer is right then we should not explain these features in terms of a disagreement about moral facts.

Why be an emotivist?

First, because emotivism denies that there are moral properties it does not need to explain what moral properties are, or where they exist or how we come to know about them. In this sense, it is a simpler theory.

A second advantage links to what we said at the end of the previous chapter. It seems that in order for a moral judgement to be genuine it has to motivate us. If you judge that vegetarianism is right but say "But what's that got to do with me?", we might think you haven't really understood the term "right". Moral judgements seem to have an action-guiding feature somehow built in to them (we discuss this in more detail in Chapter 8). Yet if moral judgements *are* expressions of beliefs – if cognitivism is right – then moral judgements do not seem able to capture this feature.

For example, I may believe that for every dollar loaned to African countries, African countries have to pay the West three dollars, but this does not motivate me to do anything; I may believe that there is a boy being bullied at my daughter's school but this does not motivate me. But contrast this with emotions. For example, if I am angry at the fact that for every dollar loaned to African countries, African countries pay back the West three dollars, then I am likely to *do* something; if I am furious about the bullying, I am likely to visit the school. It seems on the face of it that if emotivism is right and moral judgements are genuinely expressions of emotions then emotivism can account for why moral judgements move us. This is a second advantage.

In summary, by using both the OQA and his verification principle, Ayer arrives at the claim that moral judgements are expressions of emotions. It follows that he thinks moral judgements are not truth-apt and consequently there can be no genuine moral disagreements.

Emotivism is attractive because it is simpler than realist theories and helps to explain the practical nature of morality. That said, most metaethicists reject Ayer's emotivism, so let us consider why.

Does the verification principle pass the verification test?

Using the verification principle, Ayer argued that both metaphysical and theological sentences are meaningless. Claims such as "Jesus is the light of the world" and "Time is not real" are neither potentially empirically verifiable nor analytically true. They are nonsense equivalent to "Blah, bon, do, don, wobble, flip-flop, flom".

The problem is that the verification principle seems to undermine itself. Consider the statement "if a claim is neither empirically verifiable nor analytic it is meaningless". Is *this* statement empirically verifiable or analytic? It is hard to see how it could be. It does not seem that any empirical evidence would count in its favour and nor does it seem analytic. So this means that if the claim "if a claim is neither empirically verifiable nor analytic it is meaningless" is true, then it is itself meaningless. However, if we want to dig in our heels and still maintain "if a claim is neither empirically verifiable nor analytic it is meaningless" is meaningful, then the claim is false. For there is at least one claim, namely "if a claim is neither empirically verifiable nor analytic it is meaningless", which is neither empirically verifiable nor analytic but is still meaningful.

There are possible ways of defending the verification principle and debates have raged since the principle was first introduced (see e.g. Wright 1989). Perhaps the verification principle *is* analytic? Or perhaps we cannot help accepting the verification principle because it is a precondition of language use. The point is that further argument is needed, or we shall lose the key reason for Ayer's rejection of cognitivism. In the next section we shall consider why Ayer thinks moral claims *are* meaningful even though they fail the verification test.

Is Ayer really entitled to hold that moral claims are meaningful?

Is Ayer's argument that moral statements are meaningful even though they fail the verification test a flat-out contradiction of the verification principle? The rough idea seems to be that in some sense moral statements pass the verification test. Ayer thinks that moral statements fail at one level but pass at another. For instance, "torture is wrong" fails the verification test because it is neither empirically verifiable nor analytic. Yet it is not meaningless, because the feelings it expresses and the moral feelings it is calculated to provoke are verifiable.

Of course, this shifts the problem to a different level. The question we are now faced with is whether these *moral feelings* can be verified. Miller (1998) argues that they cannot, for consider how we might empirically verify a peculiarly moral feeling, that is, as a feeling expressed by a moral claim. To do this we might reflect on what it feels like when we are making moral claims. Perhaps in doing this we might come to recognize and identify a moral feeling associated with certain moral claims and hence have a method of verifying those moral feelings. However, this approach will not work. It feels different when we judge that, for example, downloading music is wrong and when we judge that mugging someone is wrong. There are no consistent feelings that we can recognize as matching each of our moral terms.

Perhaps instead by considering what people *do* we could empirically verify moral feelings? This has some plausibility, since arguably we could verify claims about non-moral feelings in this way. For example, if Jones is crying this may empirically verify the claim that "Jones is sad" or if Jones is jumping for joy this may empirically verify the claim that "Jones is happy". However, when considering moral claims this is also a non-starter. What, after all, are the outward manifestations of, for instance, "killing is wrong", or "dictatorships are unjust", or "withholding the right of asylum is morally repugnant"? There are no identifiable outward manifestations associated with judging that something is wrong, unjust, or morally repugnant. Behaviour associated with moral terms cannot be used to verify moral feelings.

If we cannot verify moral feelings through reflection or through observing outward behaviour, then it seems that Ayer has run out of options and thus moral feelings are unverifiable and moral terms *are* meaningless.

To finish the chapter we shall pre-empt some common mistakes associated with non-cognitivism and in so doing will see why emotivism may have more going for it than we first thought.

Emotivism, subjectivism and relativism

Emotivism is *not* a form of subjectivism. Subjectivism is the view that, for example, the judgement "murder is wrong" *means*, "I *disapprove of murder"*; or "freeing political prisoners is right" *means "I approve of freeing political prisoners"*. If the subjectivist is correct then when we make moral judgements we are describing our own psychological states, in this case disapproval and approval.

This is not the same as emotivism. Emotivism is a non-cognitivist theory, which means that when we make moral judgements we are *not* describing anything. Emotivism is *not* the view that in making moral judgements we are *describing* some feature of ourselves; rather, when we judge, for example, that "murder is wrong", the emotivist claims that we are expressing our disapproval towards murder. For the subjectivist, moral judgements report something; for the emotivist, moral judgements express something.

Making this distinction explicit means that we can show that emotivism is *not* a form of moral relativism. Moral relativism will be considered in more detail in Chapter 7. For now, we can take the relativist to be someone who claims that:

> ethical truth is somehow relative to a background body of doctrine, or theory, or form of life or "whirl of organism". It is an expression of the idea that there is no one true body of doctrine in ethics. There are different views, and some are "true for" some people, while others are true for others.   (Blackburn 2000: 38)

If relativism is correct, I could say "murder is wrong" and Bill could say "murder is right" and *both* of us could be correct. However, relativism is not a consequence of emotivism but rather a consequence of subjectivism. We can consider the last example in terms of subjectivism. For the subjectivist, when I say "murder is wrong", *I mean* "I disapprove of murder" and when Bill says the same thing, he means *he* approves of murder. Consequently, if I disapprove of murder and Bill approves of it we can both be speaking truthfully. But as we have seen, emotivism is not committed to subjectivism and hence emotivism can avoid the charge of relativism.

The lack of moral truth may be deemed problematic for emotivists and this will be considered in the next section. The point here though is that emotivism is not a form of subjectivism and consequently it can avoid the charge of relativism.

Emotivism and moral truth

Intuitively truth seems tied to what is real. If I say "It is raining", intuitively what makes this true is the fact that it *is* raining. If my exclamation that "I've just spilt my coffee on my laptop!" is true, then this is because I have indeed just knocked my coffee over my laptop. This suggests that pre-theoretically we accept the *correspondence theory of truth*: roughly, the view that there is a property of truth that judgements have if they *correspond with the world* (for more detail see Engel [2002]).

The correspondence theory of truth is the view of truth that has been operating in this book thus far. If we accept it and accept emotivism then moral judgements cannot be truth-apt, for emotivists think that moral judgements do not describe anything and so cannot correspond or fail to correspond to anything.

What this shows is that the emotivist could adopt a different theory of truth and in so doing could open the way for moral claims to be true or false. *Minimalism about truth* is the most popular alternative account of truth among non-cognitivists. Such an account is minimal because on such an account a claim could be true even though there is no fact that makes it so. Strictly speaking, for the minimalist the answer to "What makes moral claims true?" is "nothing". For the minimalist about truth, "murder is wrong is true" just means murder is wrong, and asking whether murder is wrong is just asking whether we should accept that murder is wrong. Adopting minimalism about truth allows the emotivist to talk about moral claims being true. We shall discuss minimalism about truth and minimalism about truth-aptness in Chapter 6.

However, there is a problem here for the emotivist. Above we said that the emotivist could avoid the charge of relativism by pointing out that moral claims are not true. Yet in this section we have shown that by rejecting the correspondence theory of truth the emotivist could talk about moral claims being true. There may then be a dilemma for the emotivist: if they want to avoid relativism then they have to abandon moral truth; if they want to account for moral truth then they are relativists.

Conclusion

Morality moves us and emotions move us. Consequently, emotivism, the view that moral judgements express emotions, can capture the practicality of morality. It can do so while side-stepping questions about what moral properties and facts might be and how we might know about them.

Emotivism claims that language dupes us into thinking that cognitivism and realism are correct when they are not. This means that in deciding whether to defend or abandon emotivism we should make a decision about how to pursue metaethics. Are we happy to give weight to a theory such as emotivism, even if this commits us to the claim that people are mistaken about what is going on in their moral talk? Or rather, should we place more weight on the fact that in our everyday talk people talk as if cognitivism and realism are correct? As we shall see in Chapter 6, the story of the development of *non-cognitivism* is the story of trying to find a path through these two desiderata: the theory and the practice.

However, emotivism is not the only theory to depart from our every-day moral talk. *Error theory* claims that *all* our moral judgements are systematically and uniformly false. When we say that "killing is wrong" or "giving money to charity is right" then we are speaking falsely. We shall spend the next chapter thinking about this radical-sounding position.

> **THINGS TO REMEMBER**
>
> - Emotivism is *not* the view that when we make moral judgements we are describing our emotions, or any other mental states.
> - The verification principle is about *meaning*, not truth.
> - Emotivism is *not* a form of relativism or subjectivism.
> - Ayer thinks that moral claims *are* meaningful.
> - The emotivist is *not* simply someone who thinks morality is more emotional than the cognitivist. Cognitivists think emotions can play a central role in morality, but that expressing emotions is not the primary role of moral judgement.
> - Everyone accepts that there are *some* expressive uses of language, but emotivists argue that moral language should be understood in this way as well.

Further reading

The classic statement of emotivism can be found in Ayer ([1936] 1974: ch. 6). The other key emotivist is Stevenson (1937, 1944). Hare (1952) develops the emotivist theory to *prescriptivism*. Rogers (2000) writes an excellent informative fun bibliography of Ayer's life. Miller (1998) discusses the verification principle in relation to emotive meaning. Miller (2003: ch. 2) gives a good survey of the issues surrounding emotivism. For a good general discussion of logical positivism see Ayer (1959) and Miller (2007: ch. 3). For an extended and subtle discussion surrounding moral disagreement see Tersman (2006). For a good survey of accounts of truth see Engel (2002: ch. 1). For clear discussion of the development of non-cognitivism see Schroeder (2010: chs 1, 2).

3

Error theory

There seems to me no doubt that our ethical judgments all claim objectivity;
but this claim, to my mind, makes them all false.   (Russell [1922] 1999: 123)

There are no objective values.   (Mackie 1977: 10)

CHAPTER AIMS
- To explain why error theory adopts cognitivism.
- To explain why Mackie rejects objective values.
- To outline some worries about error theory.
- To outline some implications of error theory.

Introduction

In this chapter we shall discuss John Mackie's error theory as put forward in his *Ethics: Inventing Right and Wrong* (1977). He argues that:

1. Moral judgements express beliefs and are truth-apt
   (*cognitivism*).
2. There are no objective moral values (*non-realism*).

This leads him to claim that:

3. All moral judgements are systematically and uniformly false.

We shall consider these claims in turn and then discuss a number of
problems arising from Mackie's account.

John L. Mackie (1917–1981)

- 1967–1981: Fellow of University College, Oxford.
- Key text: *Ethics: Inventing Right and Wrong* (1977).
- Defends error theory, the view that (i) moral judgements describe the world as containing objective moral values but (ii) the world does not contain such things. Consequently, all our moral judgements are systematically and uniformly false.

Why be a cognitivist?

Error theorists find cognitivism attractive partly because they find non-cognitivism so unattractive. Richard Joyce, an error theorist and a fictionalist, writes that non-cognitivism "smacks of interpreting a discourse in an eccentric manner simply to avoid philosophical difficulties" (Joyce forthcoming: 3), and that non-cognitivism:

> fails to adequately satisfy certain metaethical desiderata. It has trouble accounting for the authority of morality: If S's utterance of "Stealing is morally forbidden" amounts to no more than an expression of S's feelings ("Boo to stealing!") then why should anyone who is not antecedently inclined to care about S's feelings pay any attention? (*Ibid.*)

In contrast, cognitivism does not require an interpretation of moral discourse as it can arguably respect our talk of truth, falsity and disagreement, and can account for the authority of morality. Consequently this also means that cognitivism is not, whereas non-cognitivism is, challenged by the Frege–Geach problem (see Chapter 6). This suggests a motivation for cognitivism – but then why reject the existence of objective moral values? Mackie has three challenges to realism, which we shall call *relativity*, *queerness* and *epistemology*.

The challenge from relativity

Mackie challenges the moral realist to explain why, if there are objective moral values, different people, groups and cultures have different moral codes. For example, the Mafioso thinks it abominable to dishonour his family but thinks nothing of executing a snitch; in some cultures it is acceptable to rape women and commit infanticide, although clearly these are not acts that we in the West would describe as acceptable. If then there are objective moral values, how can we explain this divergence in views?

The moral realist may look to science, for we are realists about scientific facts, but there is also a multitude of different scientific beliefs; for example, there is debate about whether antimatter exists, about which is the best theory regarding the start of the universe, about how flagellum on cells evolved and so on. However, this analogy with science, rather than helping the error theorist, merely highlights the force of Mackie's challenge. For although there is a variety of views in science, we think that if people knew all the facts and reasoned correctly then they would agree. Yet the same is not true in the moral case. Arguably, in the moral case two people can agree on all the facts and reason correctly but *still* have different moral views.

For example, if Dr Smith and Dr Jones agree on all the facts about abortion and both reason correctly, it still seems possible that they could have different views on whether abortion is morally acceptable. The realist needs to explain how, if there are objective moral values, people with full information and similar reasoning powers can still disagree. In the next sections we consider two further challenges to the realist: *queerness* and *epistemology*.

What would moral values be like if they existed?

Imagine we are discussing Father Christmas with a child but she is unconvinced that he exists. She might try to work out whether he does by asking what Father Christmas is like. Is he tall, short, loud, fat, thin, bearded, dressed in green or red? It is only once the child has some idea of what Father Christmas would be like if he did exist that she could start her search.

Mackie takes a similar approach when thinking about morality. If we want to find out whether objective moral values do indeed exist, we first need to ask what we mean by moral values. Mackie's queerness challenge is that we can only conclude that there are no moral values once we have understood what they would have to be like. So what does Mackie think people mean by moral values?

METAETHICS

The first feature of our description of moral values is that they would be *independent* from our beliefs. For example, imagine the moral judgement that giving money to the arms trade is wrong. We do not believe that this would suddenly become right if enough people believed it was. We say things such as "*despite* what people think, giving money to the arms trade is wrong".

Second, moral values need to be *accessible* to us. It is no good claiming that moral values exist but that they are unknowable and inaccessible.

Third, if moral values existed they would have to be capable of giving us *reason to act* in certain ways. For example, if seal clubbing is wrong, then that is a reason not to do it; if giving to charity is right, then that is a reason to give money to charity. We have to be careful here, however, not to miss Mackie's point.

Imagine that it is morally wrong to hack into the university's computer system and change all your marks to 90 per cent. Because we have assumed that it is wrong, we can say that that is a reason not to do it. Now the odd thing about *moral* reasons is that they seem insensitive to what we desire. For example, imagine we said to the vice chancellor of the university that we really *wanted* to do well. The vice chancellor might shrug her shoulders and say, "So? What does that have to do with anything?" The point is that wanting 90 per cent does not alter the fact that we have a reason not to hack into the computer system. The reason-giving aspect of moral values seems binding on us *irrespective of our desires*. But if this is right, where does the reason-giving feature of moral values reside? Mackie thinks it must be part of the *value itself*:

> An objective good would be sought by anyone who was acquainted with it, not because of any contingent fact that this person, or every person, is so constituted that he *desire this end*, but just because the end has to-be-pursuedness somehow *built into it*.   (1977: 40, emphasis added)

If all this is right, Mackie has a description of what moral values would be like if they existed: they would have to be *independent* from us, *accessible* to us and have some *intrinsic reason-giving feature*. The next section considers Mackie's claim that if moral values have to be like this then they do not exist.

42

Queerness: why are there no objective moral values?

Mackie claims that moral values do not exist. His reasoning is that "If there were [objective moral values] then they would be entities or qualities or relations of a *very strange sort, utterly different* from anything else in the universe" (1977: 38, emphasis added).

Reading this quotation for the first time, we might be decidedly unimpressed! It does not sound particularly sophisticated or convincing. Judging something "queer", "strange" or "utterly different" does not mean that we should think it does not exist.

In the quotation above Mackie makes two claims. One is about "strangeness"; the other about being "utterly different from anything in the universe". These are distinct. Focusing on "strangeness" is not helpful; for example, dowsing seems strange and the controversial collapse of tower block 7 after the terrorist attack on the Twin Towers of the World Trade Center was strange but this does not lead to doubts about the existence of dowsing or collapsing buildings.

We can read Mackie as claiming that moral values, if they existed, would have to be "utterly different" from anything else in the universe. At first, this does not seem much better. After all, it seems that I am different from anything in the universe: I am unique. Presumably we can also think of many other things, besides people, that are "utterly different" – a duck-billed platypus for example. Yet this does not throw the existence of me or the duck-billed platypus into doubt.

The way to understand Mackie's point is to note the word "utterly" in "utterly different". Although in some sense I am different, I am not *utterly* different from anything else in the universe. I have many features in common with other things: I am a human being, I have legs, arms and metabolize my food. The duck-billed platypus is different – it lays eggs, is venomous and is a mammal – but it is not "utterly different". After all, other creatures have each of these qualities. However, if Mackie is right then moral values would have to be *utterly* different and he thinks *this* throws their existence into doubt.

Why does Mackie think this? On first consideration, the fact that moral values would have to be independent, accessible and give us reason for action does not seem "utterly different". Consider the coffee machine in the philosophy department. If I am thirsty then I have a reason to go to the staff room; it is an accessible fact that the staff room contains the coffee machine; and when I am sipping coffee at home I still believe that there is a coffee machine at work. It seems we have a fact – that there is a coffee machine in the staff room – with the features Mackie identified as being characteristic of moral values: its existence is *independent* from what we think, we can come to *know about* the coffee machine, and it can give us *reasons to act*. But we do not think coffee machines are utterly different from anything in the universe, and they certainly exist. What is going on?

The reason that moral values are, and coffee machines are not, utterly different is the "to-be-pursuedness" of moral values. Although it is true that the coffee machine *can* give us a reason to get a cup of coffee, this reason is dependent on whether I am thirsty. If I drink a bottle of water, it is not *still* true that I have a reason to get a drink of coffee. This contrasts with moral values. Mackie thinks if moral values existed they would give us a reason *irrespective* of our psychology.

Recall the example about hacking into the university computer system. Knowing it is wrong to hack into the computer system allows us to conclude that we have a reason not to do it. Importantly – unlike facts about coffee machines – we do not need to consider people's desires before we can draw this conclusion. This helps us to see why Mackie thinks moral values would be so queer.

Consider all the things we experience: they either guide us because we have certain desires (e.g. thirst and the coffee machine); or they are independent of our desires and do not guide us at all. What we have never experienced – and perhaps are unable to make sense of – is something that has both these features at the same time. How can something both be independent from us and also give us reason to behave in a particular way? Mackie's point is that given our description of moral values, if they existed, then they would have to be like this. He therefore concludes that we have good reason to think that moral values do not exist.

We now have two challenges to moral realism: the challenge from the variety of moral views and the challenge from queerness. Mackie's final challenge is to suggest that we could never know about moral values even if they did exist.

The epistemological argument: even if there were moral values we could not know about them

Mackie's third challenge to realism is a consequence of his queerness argument. Recall that it is part of the "job description" of moral values that they are accessible. Yet if moral values are "utterly different from anything in the universe", then Mackie thinks that our way of accessing them would have to be utterly different from any normal ways of accessing things. Mackie thinks that if moral values were queer, then the only way to access them would be via a special faculty, which he calls a "moral intuition". As he puts it:

> [N]one of our ordinary accounts of sensory perception or introspection or the framing and confirming of explanatory hypotheses or inference or logical construction or conceptual analysis, or any combination of these, will provide a satisfactory answer [to how we might access moral values].
>
> (1977: 39)

However, he thinks that to postulate a special faculty would be a "travesty of actual moral thinking" that would demonstrate an unwillingness to engage in mature philosophical conversation (although unfortunately he does not explain why).

Thus, for Mackie, we can not only reject the existence of objective moral values but also claim that even if they did exist we could never come to know about them! But the ability to know about them – we agreed – is an essential part of what it is to be a moral value. Consequently, we have excellent grounds to reject realism.

Are moral judgements systematically and uniformly false?

Let us now put the parts we have discussed together. Moral judgements express beliefs that are about objective moral values (cognitivism) and there are good reasons to suppose that objective moral values do not exist (non-realism). But if there is nothing corresponding to our moral judgements, then those judgements are all false.

Mackie is not claiming that any sentence that includes a moral term is false. For example, "all judgements of the form 'x is wrong' will be

45

false" would be *true*. The claim is rather that all moral assertions are systematically and uniformly false.

Moral error theory is a radical position. It is the view that all these statements are *false*:

- Abducting and torturing children is morally wrong.
- Providing famine relief to starving families is morally good.
- Locking people in a church and throwing petrol bombs through the window is evil.
- It is morally right to save the boy trapped in floodwaters.

The error theorist would be quick to remind us that he is not saying that it is *right* to torture children, *bad* to give money to charity, *wrong* to save a boy trapped in floodwaters. For he argues that there is no moral truth at all. Even so, it seems that error theory goes completely against how we talk and think. Indeed, we might believe that if Mackie's reasoning has led us to such a conclusion then there must be something wrong with it (this line of thought is pursued below). However, before this we shall consider a different question.

If all moral claims are false, then why be moral?

If we have read Mackie and come to believe that all our moral claims are false, what should we do? More importantly, why not just give up on moral talk altogether? Mackie's answer is essentially that we should carry on believing in morality – despite it being false – because to do so serves a *purpose*. In particular, it regulates relationships, controls people's behaviour and helps us to resist temptations and feel safe. The error theorist can think of morality as the glue needed in order for society to operate; glue that would lose its stickiness if the illusion of moral truth vanished. Error theory holds that moral practice is justified through its usefulness, not through its truthfulness.

This raises some fascinating issues about the value of morality, which we shall consider when we discuss fictionalism in Chapter 10. We shall now examine some arguments against error theory that are by no means exhaustive but provide a taste of some key issues.

How much does Mackie rely on everyday moral talk and how much does he ignore it?

There seems to be a conflict in the error theorist's methodology. Consider again a quotation that we saw in part at the start of the first section of this chapter: "What makes many ... error theorists ... uneasy about the noncognitivist's response is that it smacks of interpreting a discourse in an eccentric manner simply to avoid philosophical difficulties" (Joyce forthcoming: 3). Hence error theory accepts cognitivism in part because it respects the face value of our moral practice. But if the idea is to *start* from everyday talk then it seems the error theorist may have a problem.

After all, there is not only a presumptive argument in favour of cognitivism: there is a presumptive argument in favour of *realism* and in favour of *truth*. Most people say things like "It is a *fact* that killing is wrong", or "It is *true* that taking hostages is bad". So, if the error theorist's starting point is how people talk then it seems *ad hoc* to favour cognitivism rather than realism or moral truth.

Furthermore, from how people talk there seems to be evidence *against* what Mackie calls the to-be-pursuedness of moral values. Imagine that someone promised to meet a friend at the pub but becomes clinically depressed; as a result, they have no time for promises, friends and pubs. Do we think this person still has a reason to go to the pub? The error theorist would say that if keeping promises is a good thing to do, then yes, the person has a reason because goodness has a reason-giving force "built into it". But I suspect it is not as clear-cut as this (these issues will be explored in more detail when normative and motivating reasons are discussed in Chapter 8). Rather, many people may think that because the person is depressed he has ceased to have a reason to keep his promise. This sort of example suggests that the reason-giving nature of moral values is *not* insensitive to the contingencies of people's psychology. Consequently, on surveying how people think and talk, if moral values existed they would not have to have a to-be-pursuedness built into them. This would remove the main claim regarding the queerness of moral values.

This is not a substantial argument but it is a challenge in a form of a question to the error theorist: namely, who do you listen to when trying to formulate the *description* of moral values?

However, even if Mackie can respond to this challenge and navigate a way through this methodological worry, there are further problems.

Challenging the queerness argument: what's wrong with being queer?

> My own suspicion is that the universe is not only queerer than we suppose, but queerer than we "can" suppose.
>
> (Haldane 1928: 10)

Imagine for the sake of argument that after years of contemplation you decide that Platonism is true and that you believe the Form of the Good exists (see *Republic* 508c–509a). Therefore, when Mackie describes moral values as objective, accessible and intrinsically action-guiding, you say, "Yes, that's what I believe."

How, then, is Mackie going to argue against you? It is hard to see what Mackie might say besides, "Well, the Form of the Good you talk about is 'utterly different from anything in the universe'." But this, of course, you knew! In fact, it seems reasonable to think that Platonism is attractive for that very reason; one might think, for example, that the fact that it is utterly different helps one to respect the uniqueness and the gravitas of morality.

What, then, is going on in Mackie's argument? Well, in part, Mackie is presupposing naturalism. We defined naturalism as the view that the only things that could exist are those that the natural sciences or psychology are happy to deal with. With this in place, it *may be* plausible to conclude that moral values, as Mackie conceives them, do not exist. After all, presumably the scientific picture of the world does not contain things which have this "to-be-pursuedness" built into them. But in making this assumption explicit we can see that Mackie's queerness argument is only as good as his defence of naturalism.

Challenging the queerness argument: McDowell on Mackie's presumption that "real" means mind-independent

Roughly put, Mackie's argument is something like this:

1. If moral values are *real*, then they are *mind-independent*; that is, they would exist even if people did not.
2. But this would be too queer, and consequently moral values cannot be mind-independent.

Therefore

3. Moral values cannot be real.

John McDowell (1998) has argued against this type of reasoning by challenging (1). He argues that moral values could be real but also mind-dependent. To do this he looks for *companions in innocence*. In particular, he asks us to think about secondary qualities such as colour.

Consider the colours on the Olympic rings. Are these real? It seems that they are. If someone says "one of the rings is purple", we might retort "no, you are wrong: it is red". That is to say, we talk and think as if it is a *genuine fact* that the ring is red. It follows that if Mackie's line of argument is right – specifically if we grant (1) – then, given that colours are real, they would have to be mind-independent.

However, this seems implausible. Do we think that the rings on the Olympic flag are red, blue, green, yellow and black in and of themselves? That is, could we make sense of this claim about their colour without any reference to people's perceptions? Arguably not, for when we say that one of the rings is red what we mean is that the ring would look red to a normal perceiver under normal conditions.

Notice we could still stay that even if humans ceased to exist the ring would be red, because this is just to say that *if* people did exist they would judge the ring as being red. Therefore, a claim about something being coloured seemingly will have to make reference to people's perceptions of colour. Colours, then, appear to be mind-*dependent*.

We have arrived at two views that, if the reasoning in Mackie's argument is correct, are in conflict: first, that colours are real; and second, that colours are mind-dependent. McDowell's solution is to claim there is no conflict at all by giving up Mackie's assumption that if something is real then it has to be mind-independent. If McDowell is right then we have space to argue that moral values may only exist because people do, but still maintain that they are real.

We need to say a little more about this. If McDowell were claiming that everything that is dependent on our minds is real then his view would be silly. After all, the hallucinations someone might have on an LSD trip are directly dependent on her mind but although the hallucinations are real, the *things* she hallucinates are not. Consequently what McDowell needs is a way of distinguishing between things that are *not* real, such as hallucinations, and things that are real, such as value. He does this by looking to how we experience and talk about hallucinations and values.

For example, we do not talk as if Hendrix floating over the sofa exists independently of our experience. We do not think that when the drugs are out of our system Hendrix will *still* be there. Whereas, if we think that torture is wrong we *do* talk as if it is wrong despite what we or anyone may think. That is to say, in our moral talk we make space between how something *seems*, and how something *is*, whereas when talking about hallucinations we do not.

Furthermore, moral values seem to be experienced differently from hallucinations. If we see someone kicking a cat, the wrongness of the act seems to be somehow "*there to be experienced*" (McDowell 1985). Now contrast this with seeing a hallucination. In this case what we hallucinate is not experienced as part of the world. To put this another way, the phenomenology of hallucination seems to direct the mind's eye *inwards*, whereas the phenomenology of moral experience seems to direct the mind's eye *outwards* into the world. Of course this is crude and metaphorical, and McDowell spends a lot of time trying to make more of these sorts of suggestions. However, it at least starts to develop a way of distinguishing mind-dependent real from mind-dependent not-real. This in turn allows us to demarcate values from such things as hallucinations, which supports the claim that moral values can be mind-dependent but still real.

Finally, one should be wary of reading too much into the analogy with secondary qualities, which is introduced simply to highlight the point about reality and mind-dependence. McDowell and other theorists who take this line – sometimes called sensibility theorists – do not, for example, think we can perceive value just as we can perceive colour. And whereas we think that something is red if and only if a normal agent judges it red under normal conditions, this is not adequate for the moral account. For instance, McDowell introduces the idea of a *merited* response from people when trying to make sense of how value is dependent on people (McDowell 1998).

To conclude, if McDowell is right, then the reality of moral values may be dependent on our emotions and attitudes, but this does not make them any less real. In particular, we should not think that mind-dependence leads, without argument, to the claim that moral value is mere projection or mere illusion. We can then reject Mackie's line of reasoning because moral value would be less queer than he thought.

This, though, needs much more explanation and defence than there is room for here.

Challenging the argument from queerness: a Moorean shift

Finally, there could be a more direct way of challenging the error theorist. This approach takes seriously the thought that if our reasoning leads to the conclusion that all moral judgements are systematically and uniformly false, then there is something wrong with our reasoning.

This argumentative strategy has come to be known as the "Moorean Shift", after Moore. Moore first deployed this strategy in *epistemology* against those who believe we cannot know anything about the external world (Moore 1939). After a series of arguments, the sceptic claims that we do not know the things we thought we knew about the external world. We do not know we have two hands; that there is a cat at the end of the garden; or that there is a sun in the sky. Moore thinks that if scepticism leads to this sort of conclusion then we have reason to reject scepticism. He argues like this:

1. I know that I have two hands, that there is a cat in the garden, a sun in the sky.
2. If the sceptic is correct then I cannot know I have two hands, that there is a cat in the garden, a sun in the sky.

Therefore,

3. There is a problem with the sceptic's argument.

This argument is valid, although whether it is sound remains to be seen. The suggestion is that we may be able to deploy this form of argument against error theory. Here is how it might run:

1. "Boiling children in oil for fun is morally wrong" is true.
2. If error theory is correct, "Boiling children in oil for fun is morally wrong" is not true.

Therefore,

3. There is a problem with error theory.

This again is *valid*, but of course, we now have to decide whether to take the truth of moral claims or the truth of error theory. This will primarily depend on what rational grounds there are for accepting the truth of the claim that boiling children for fun is wrong over error theory. For instance, we might think that it is at least as rational to believe we can know that some moral claims are true as it is to believe that no moral claims are true – in which case this Moorean Shift approach would challenge the error theorist.

Conclusion

Error theory in morality derives from three plausible views. The first is *cognitivism*, the view that moral judgements express beliefs and aim to describe some sector of reality and are consequently truth-apt. The second is *non-realism*, the view that there are no moral values that correspond to our moral beliefs. The third is that truth involves correspondence to facts. These three views lead to the radical conclusion that moral claims are systematically and uniformly false. When discussing this further, we could question cognitivism, non-realism or the correspondence theory of truth; however, we shall conclude with a general observation.

In the Introduction we characterized metaethics as *descriptive* and as having no direct normative implications. I suggested that the metaethicist is like a football pundit, rather than a player or referee. Metaethics tries to adequately capture what we are doing when we are being moral. However, error theory puts pressure on this characterization, for it seems naive to think that learning that all our moral claims are false would not have a direct impact on us as moral agents. Accepting error theory seems to lead to the pressing question "What ought we to do now?" And this is a *normative* question.

However we end up answering this, error theory seems to demand some response, which in turn raises interesting questions about the relationship between normative ethics and metaethics.

Many philosophers think that error theory should only be adopted as a last resort. Consequently they may argue for the existence of moral properties and the truth of moral claims. In the next chapter we discuss what such a realist position might look like.

THINGS TO REMEMBER

- Cognitivism is the view that moral judgements are *truth-apt*, and not the claim that they are *true*.
- Even if error theory is true we can construct sentences that contain moral terms but are still true, for example "All judgements that killing is wrong are false".
- It is the *intrinsic* nature of the to-be-pursuedness that is meant to be queer.
- Real does not have to mean mind-independent.
- Mackie does not think we should stop being moral; error theory is not a licence for stealing, killing and so on.
- Mackie does not think we can reject realism because people have different moral views. He is making the weaker claim that different moral views present a *challenge* to realism.

Further reading

Mackie's views are spelled out in Mackie (1977: chs 1, 5). For a good survey and discussion see Miller (2003: ch. 6). Error theory is making a comeback of late: see Joyce & Kirchin (2010: esp. "Against Ethics"), and Daly & Liggins (2010). For a classic debate about the "queerness" of moral properties see Brink (1984) and Garner (1990). For good debate about modern error theory see Finlay (2008) and Joyce (forthcoming). For a sustained defence of error theory see Joyce (2001).

4

Moral realism and naturalism

[I]f there ever was a consensus of understanding about "realism", as a philosophical term of art, it has undoubtedly been fragmented by the pressures exerted by the various debates – so much so that a philosopher who asserts that she is a realist about theoretical science, for example, or ethics, has probably, for most philosophical audiences, accomplished little more than to clear her throat.   (Wright: 1992: 1)

CHAPTER AIMS
- To explain moral realism.
- To explain the attractions of naturalistic versions of moral realism.
- To outline a presumptive argument in favour of moral realism.
- To explain the distinction between analytic and synthetic realism.

Introduction

Moral realists are cognitivists – although, as Mackie has shown us, not all cognitivists are realists. To be a moral realist is to think that moral properties are real and that these properties are in some sense *independent* from what people think, believe and judge. Yet what is it to say that a moral property is real? At first it seems a rather odd claim because if we think of things that seem unquestionably real (at least to non-philosophers) such as tables or footballs or street lights, it would be bizarre to think that moral properties were in the same class of things as these. It is not as if we could bump into wrongness on the way to work, or as if rightness could obscure our view of the sunset, or goodness might get caught in the lift, or badness interfere with our television reception. In fact, many people are turned off moral realism precisely because they cannot make sense of what the reality of moral properties might be.

However, a little reflection shows that this rejection of the reality of moral properties by analogy to tables, street lights and so on would be far too hasty. To see why, consider whether these things are real:

- Love
- Society
- The equator
- Numbers
- Protons
- Time

If you answered "yes" to some of these things then it seems that we need to think a bit harder about what "real" might mean. After all, even if we think protons are real, we do not actually "bump up against them". We do not smell them or see them and they do not directly interfere with our progress through the world. Or again, considering our list, arguably the equator is real, yet planes do not have to fly higher in order to avoid it. So those people who think that moral properties cannot possibly be real because such a thing would be too odd should consider the above list and ask themselves what calling something "real" actually commits us to. The list shows that what we think is real extends far beyond footballs, tables and street lighting. Calling moral properties real might then not be as odd as it first may seem, and this is a theme that we shall keep returning to in this chapter. A starting-point in considering the reality of moral properties can be found in how we think and talk.

A presumptive argument in favour of realism

Independence

When we make moral claims we talk as if whether something is right or wrong, good or bad is beyond our interests and preferences. This is in contrast with claims about taste. Consider an example to illustrate this contrast.

Imagine we are trying to decide which television programme to watch. You want to watch *American Idol* and I think that *The Simpsons* would be better. After a discussion we might have to agree to disagree and flip a coin. Although we have our preferences for certain programmes we are not particularly offended or bothered with one choice over another.

However, now imagine that you have acquired a video of a lecturer attacking a student for forgetting to hand in an essay. You suggest that we put it online for the world to see. I judge that this would be morally wrong but you do not see it this way. Notice that in this instance a mere preference is not going to decide whether it is right to put the video on the web. In this case I certainly would not be happy to flip a coin on it and I certainly am bothered if you get your way. The mere fact that you really want to show it because you think many people will think it is very funny does not make me change my mind at all.

How can we explain this way of thinking and talking? Well, we would expect to talk and think this way if moral properties really did exist. If moral realism were correct and there were genuine moral properties then this could explain why we think moral judgments might be insensitive to preferences and desires and mass opinion. Consider another feature of our moral practice: convergence.

Convergence

Arguably there has been and continues to be convergence on moral views and this is best explained by the existence of moral properties. Consider an example.

Imagine we lock fifty top forensic scientists into fifty individual labs with no way of communicating. Then we give them a gun that has recently been fired in a crime and ask them to give us as much information as they can from this piece of evidence. I suspect they would be in agreement in what they suggest. Of course, there will be some differences but there will also be convergence. For example, all might agree that the bloodstain on the handle was type O-negative, that the bullets were hollow-tipped and that there was DNA on the firing mechanism. How might we go about explaining this convergence in evidence? Well, one explanation – although not a particularly good one – is that the agreement was a massive fluke. All the scientists just happened to say the same thing because there was some sort of cosmic accident.

This is not an attractive explanation and more naturally we might say that the reason there is agreement about certain answers is because the gun had certain properties. The blood on the gun had the property of being type O-negative, the bullets had the property of being hollow-tipped and so on. So a good explanation for why there is a convergence in views is that there are some properties that people come to recognize.

Now consider another example. Imagine we put fifty people from around the world in individual rooms and ask them to think up the ten most important *moral* rules. Again, I suspect that there will be a large amount of convergence. For example, they all might write that it is wrong to steal, or wrong to kill children, or wrong to enslave people. Although the lists would not be identical there would certainly be much overlap. If this were indeed the case then we would want to look for the best explanation of why there was this convergence in moral beliefs.

A good reason would be that there really are certain moral properties and that they have been recognized by the people in the rooms. So the act of killing children has the property of being wrong, treating people as slaves has the property of being wrong and so on. Although this thought experiment clearly does not prove realism, what it does do is suggest that the idea that there really are moral properties is not as contrary to everyday thinking as it may first seem.

Truth

Consider a quotation that seems to echo an intuitive idea: "a truth, any truth, should depend for its truth on something 'outside' it, in virtue of which it is true" (Armstrong 2004: 7). Truth seems somehow bound up with what is real; for example, if the claim "my bike is muddy" is true then this is because some feature of the world makes it true; in this case, it would be true if my bike had the property of being muddy. This intuition can be more formally labelled the *truth-maker thesis*. That is, a claim is true if and only if some feature of the world, such as properties, makes it true.

Now if some moral claims are true and if the truth-maker thesis is correct then we can say that there are some features of the world that make them true. If the claim "killing politicians is morally wrong" is *true* then this would mean that there is some feature of the world – namely the wrongness of killing politicians – that makes the claim true. In the next section we shall consider some other features that will help to further build up a presumptive argument in favour of moral realism.

Disagreement, progress and phenomenology

We believe that there are genuine moral disagreements. Arguably the best explanation for this is that there are genuine moral properties. Consider an example. Imagine that I claim that late-term abortion is morally wrong but you claim it is not. Common sense tells us that we cannot both be right, and that one of us must have made a mistake. If moral realism is false and late-term abortions do not have either the property of being right or the property of being wrong, then it is hard to see why we cannot accept that we both could be right. In other words, we might think that moral realism is the best explanation for why we hold that an act cannot be both right and not-right, both good and not-good and so on.

Furthermore the fact that there is moral progress is arguably best explained in terms of moral realism. It seems undeniable that there has been some moral progress: we no longer send people up chimneys, or force children to mend looms, or keep slaves and so on. However, if there is progress this seems to imply that we are somehow moving closer to the truth of how the world actually ought to be. But if moral realism is false then it seems that there could be no standard or benchmark, and it is hard to see why we would think moral progress was possible at all.

Finally, consider the phenomenology we mentioned in the previous chapter. Our experiences as moral agents seem to support realism. For example, it seems that sometimes we are surprised by our own reactions to situations. Imagine that we thought that fox-hunting was morally acceptable and we are out with the hunt when it reaches its conclusion with a pack of dogs ripping a fox to pieces. In this instance we might change our mind about fox-hunting in a moment. Suddenly we discover through experience that it is wrong. If moral properties really do exist then this sort of revelation should not be unexpected, whereas if moral realism is false, and there are no moral properties, then it seems that this type of phenomenology would be unexpected and therefore require an explanation.

Of course, the non-realist would remain unmoved by all this. All these observations are very interesting but they do not prove anything. We could explain any one of them in ways which do not rely on the reality of moral properties. For example, perhaps the fact that we cannot think that late-term abortion is both wrong and not-wrong is just a consequence of our language use rather than evidence that late-term abortion has a moral property. Or perhaps people would not really come to converge on their views if we asked them to write their list of ten rules. Or perhaps there is no such thing as moral progress at all.

In general terms, although these observations might be evidence that there are moral properties, we might think that really they tell us about is our language use, our psychology and perhaps some social history. But this is not what we are directly interested in as realists; rather, we are interested in what is real. So it does seem that we need a more sophisticated way of defending the reality of moral properties. We shall then consider how a realist might go about doing this.

One way of demystifying moral properties would be to show that they are identical with *natural* properties: those properties that are "the subject matter of the natural sciences and also of psychology. It may be said to include all that has existed, does exist or will exist in time" (Moore [1903] 1993: 92). If the moral property of goodness is identical with pleasure then it is not odd to say that goodness is real, or that we could be wrong about whether something is good, or that we could come to recognize the good in something. Because of course it is not odd to say that pleasure is real, or that we could be wrong about whether something is pleasurable, and it is not odd to claim that we can come to know that something is pleasurable. How, though, could we secure an identity claim between moral properties and natural properties? How could we be moral realists who are naturalists?

There are two broad approaches to answering these questions. First we shall consider Frank Jackson's approach, which claims that we can establish that moral properties are natural properties through *a priori* conceptual analysis. Second we shall consider Cornell realists, who think that we can establish such an identity *a posteriori*.

Jackson's claim that moral properties are identical with natural properties

If we were to try to define moral *terms*, how might we do it? One approach may be through *a priori conceptual analysis*. But in the wake of Moore's OQA (see Chapter 1) conceptual analysis of moral terms was thought to be a dead end. However, things have changed and realists have once again turned to conceptual analysis. This is primarily due to a group of philosophers working at the Australian National University in Canberra. We shall consider how Jackson has applied what has come to be known as the "Canberra Plan" to ethics (see Jackson 1998).

Jackson's Canberra Plan: a new hope for the conceptual analysis of moral terms?

Jackson argues that we can give a *reductive* definition of moral terms – "reductive" because the definition itself does not contain any moral terms. He thinks we can do this by using an established process developed by Frank Ramsey and refined by David Lewis – a method inventively named the Ramsey–Lewis method (Lewis 1970). This application of the Ramsey–Lewis method is at the heart of the Canberra Plan.

Consider an example from Jackson *et al.* (2009). Imagine that we are trying to define "neutron", "electron" and "proton" but in a way that does not rely on any theoretical physics. This is analogous to Jackson defining "good", "right" and "wrong" without relying on any moral terms. Obviously, we cannot say things such as "a proton is whatever attracts an electron", or "a proton repels protons", for this is to use other theoretical terms. The basic Ramsey–Lewis method is to tell a story something like this:

> There is one kind of thing, and another, and yet another; instances of the first of these orbit a clump of instances of the other two; instances of the first and the second are attracted to each other; instances of the first repel each other, as do instances of the second; instances of the third exhibit no attraction or repulsion to other instances of its own kind; some strange force keeps the members of the second kind together in a clump despite their mutual repulsion; and so on. (*Ibid.*: 54)

In such an account there is *no* mention of "protons", "electrons" or "neutrons", but we can give the meaning of each of the terms by referring back to the whole story. So, for example, we can say that by "neutron" we mean whatever plays the role such that it "exhibits no attraction or repulsion to other instances of its own kind", "orbits instances of the other two things" and so on.

Consequently we can claim that if something plays the "electron", "proton" or "neutron" role in the above story then it would be an electron, proton or neutron. Jackson's thought is that we can make the same sort of moves when trying to define moral terms.

In the above example, we started with a theoretical physics "story" that specified the roles of electron, proton and neutron; in the moral case Jackson thinks we need to start with a moral "story" that specifies the roles of each moral property. To do this we must write down all the truths associated with each moral term. Jackson believes that where we pick these truths *from* is of vital importance. Crucially we cannot take them from our everyday moral practice (folk morality). Instead, we need to tell the story using the truths taken from a morality where there has been a sustained discussion and people have arrived at a consensus in their moral views. Such a morality is what Jackson calls *mature folk morality*.

We then need to construct a list of all the truths of mature folk morality, but because we are interested in realism, all these truths must be written in terms of properties. The list will contain such things as: "something cannot have the property of being both wrong and right"; "if someone said that x has the property of rightness and someone else said it does not have the property of rightness, then at least one of them is mistaken"; "if we judge that something has the property of being right then we are, all things being equal, motivated by it"; "if something has the property of wrongness that gives us reason not to pursue it". Note that it is *not* a challenge to Jackson's position that we cannot actually write such a list. Jackson's point is to suggest a method that we might use to give a successful conceptual analysis of moral terms.

Recall that Jackson is trying to give a reductive definition – that is, a definition that does not rely on any moral terms. Therefore, the next move is to remove all references to moral properties in the story. The easiest way of doing this is to give each moral property – for example right, wrong or good – a unique variable: a_r, a_w, a_g …

Thus for every instance of wrong in our story we would use, say, a_w; for every instance of right, a_r; for good, a_g. Our story would now include the sentences: "something cannot have the property of being both a_w and a_r"; "if someone said that x has a_w and someone else said it does not have a_w, then at least one of them is mistaken"; "if we judge something has the property of a_w then, all things being equal, we are motivated not to do it"; "if something has the property of a_w that gives us reason not to pursue it".

We are now in a similar position to the neutron, proton and electron story above. We have a story telling us about the role that each moral property would play in mature folk morality but with no mention of moral terms. We need to make one final point. The story has to contain enough information to pick out *one*, and *only one*, property. Jackson can claim that the reductive definition of "wrong" is the *role* a_w plays in our massive and complex functional story. The reductive definition of "right" is the role a_r plays in our massive and complex functional story, "good" is the role a_g plays in our massive and complex functional story, and so on.

Jackson can now conclude that *wrongness* is whatever property uniquely satisfies the a_w role; rightness is the property that *uniquely* satisfies the a_r role; goodness is the property that *uniquely* satisfies the a_g role and so on. Jackson can claim then that there really are moral properties and that they are identical to natural properties – the natural properties that play the role specified by the Ramsey–Lewis "story".

If Jackson is right we then have a way of giving a *reductive analytic definition* for each moral term. As he writes:

> I have now told the story about how to identify the ethical properties: find the properties which are such that, going under their purely [natural] property names, they make the clauses of mature folk morality come out true ... and then identify each ethical property with the corresponding [natural] property.   (1998: 141)

In conclusion, Jackson has offered a reductive analytic definition of moral terms. He thinks that there are real moral properties and that these are natural properties. If he is right that they are natural properties, then the supposed "mystery" of what the reality of moral properties might be dissipates.

Jackson and the open question argument

If Jackson's position is *analytic* realism then are we able to use the OQA against it? We might think it is an open question whether right is whatever occupies the "rightness" role in Jackson's "story". Further, we may think that this is enough to challenge Jackson's claim that the property of being right just is whatever fits the rightness role in the story.

Jackson believes that if we think that it is an open question whether, for example, right is whatever fits the "rightness" role, then this is because we are not part of mature folk morality. Essentially, Jackson's response to the OQA is that we find questions concerning his account open because his analysis is complex. In contrast, the mature folk would find questions about his proposed reductive account "closed".

However, we might reframe the question and challenge him again. For we might think it is possible for the mature folk to question whether, say, right is whatever occupies the rightness role. Jackson's answer to this is brief:

> It may be objected that even when all the negotiation and critical reflection is over and we have arrived at mature folk morality, it will still make perfect sense to doubt that the right is what occupies the rightness role. But now I think that we … are entitled to dig in our heels and insist that the idea that what fits the bill *that* well might still fail to be rightness, is nothing more than a hangover from the platonist conception that the meaning of a term like "right" is somehow a matter of its picking out, or being mysteriously attached to, the form of the right.   (*Ibid.*: 151)

We might remain unimpressed with this response and question what justifies Jackson's insistence on this. Is there any independent evidence that there is such a hangover other than the fact that we think mature folk might find questions concerning his account open? It is not clear to me. However, I shall leave the reader to consider further whether the OQA can be applied to Jackson's account.

In conclusion, Jackson has provided a reductive analytic definition of moral terms. He thinks that there are moral properties and that these are natural properties, and that his account is immune to the OQA. Moral properties are then real but are no more mysterious than the reality of other natural properties, such as something being pleasurable. Typically, however, moral realists do not go in for conceptual analysis but rather adopt *synthetic* realism. So let us consider why, and what such an account might be like.

Synthetic realism: introduction

The synthetic realist thinks that, despite what Jackson and other analytic realists might think, metaethics should work by speculation, hypothesis, induction, trial and error and predicted indeterminism rather than by stipulation, certainty, analyticity and conceptual analysis.

We can now look back at our list of things in the introduction. Consider the proton. Why do we think protons are real? As we said above, it is not as though we can see, smell or hear them. What right do we have to be realists about protons? The natural answer is that protons seem to have the ability to explain things. If protons were real then this would explain the movement of electrons, the reason that there is a vapour trail in the cloud chamber, why the Large Hadron Collider gives the pictures it does and so on. It seems then that we can gain the right to talk about something being real if we can show that it plays a role in explanations.

The synthetic moral realists take this line of thought. They argue that if we postulate moral properties as real, we can explain certain phenomena better than if we did not. Moral properties figure in the best explanatory accounts of the world. We can "earn the right" to talk about such things existing because they "pull their weight" in our explanations. The synthetic realist Peter Railton puts it like this:

> [The moral realist should] … postulate a realm of facts in virtue of the contribution they would make to the *a posteriori explanation* of certain features of our experience. For example, an external world is posited to explain the coherence, stability, and intersubjectivity of sense-experience. A moral realist who [wishes to benefit from] this stratagem must show that the *postulation of moral facts similarly can have an explanatory function.* (1986: 172)

What Railton is saying, then, is that we can claim the external world is real by showing that it explains certain features of our experiences very well; so we can claim moral properties are real by showing that they also explain certain features of our experiences very well.

Synthetic moral realists differ concerning how much importance they give to talk of the explanatory role of moral properties. Some, namely the Cornell realists, think that explanatory potential is *sufficient* to establish the reality of moral properties. Others, such as Railton, think that it is merely *necessary*. For the sake of argument we shall stick to the Cornell realists' view that it is sufficient. That is, we will assume that if it can be established that moral properties figure in our best explanatory accounts then moral properties are real and moral realism is correct. For more on this see Leiter (2001).

Synthetic realists and ontology: earning the right to talk about the reality of moral properties

How might this work in the moral case? In the scientific case we have a good idea of what we are trying to explain. Why do physicists believe that protons exist? Or chemists think that molecules exist? Or biologists that an organism has a certain DNA sequence? The reason is that by postulating protons, molecules and DNA they can explain things such as why a certain organism has the phenotype it does, why the metal melted at a certain temperature, why there is a certain picture generated by the Large Hadron Collider. If the synthetic moral realists want to pursue this line of thought, how is the analogy going to go? To consider an example, imagine being transported back to Namibia 1904 and being an eyewitness in this account of the genocide:

> Some distance beyond Hamakari we camped at a water hole. While there, a German soldier found a little Herero boy about nine months old lying in a bush. The child was crying. He brought it into the camp where I was. The soldiers formed a ring and started throwing it to each other and catching it as if it was a ball. The child was terrified and hurt and crying very much. After a time they got tired of this and one of the soldiers fixed his bayonet on his rifle and said he would catch the baby boy. The boy was tossed in the air towards him and as it fell he caught it and transfixed the body with the bayonet. The child died in a few minutes and the incident was greeted with roars of laughter. (Totten *et al.* 2009: 35)

On experiencing this you would, I hope, believe that what the soldiers were doing *is* wrong. It is not as if you see what is going on, then write down "bayonet", "child", "screaming", "pain" and then ponder the list, and finally draw the conclusion that it is wrong. Rather, on witnessing this atrocious act you immediately come to believe it is wrong. The key question is: what is the best explanation for why you come to believe this?

The synthetic realist would claim that there is an excellent explanation, namely that the action of bayoneting children has the property of being morally wrong. If they are right and this is a better explanation than any other of why we form the belief then they have earned the right to talk about the reality of moral properties. It would then seem that moral realism is correct.

However, when people hear this for the first time they are often unimpressed. Surely the pain of the child, laughter of the soldiers, screaming of the child and further facts about our psychology best explain why we believe the act is wrong. There is no further explanatory role for a moral property – talk of moral properties is redundant. How might the synthetic moral realist proceed?

Before we consider this challenge based on the work of Miller (2003: 145–6), we need the notion of *supervenience*. Supervenience is meant to be knowable *a priori* and is the view that two situations cannot be different in their moral properties without differing in their natural properties. Consider an example: that it is right for Laker fans to riot but wrong for Bulls fans. Someone who holds such a view is forced – on pain of incoherence – to cite some significant differences between the rioters; for example, perhaps the Laker fans had tear gas thrown at them whereas the Bulls fans did not.

This means that if our moral theory holds that the *only* reason a certain action could be wrong is if it brings about needless pain, suffering and death then, if our moral theory is right, removing the needless pain, suffering and death of an action would mean it would not be wrong. Supervenience will be looked at in more detail shortly.

If we are synthetic moral realists then it would be useful to have a test to ascertain whether or not a property does have some genuine explanatory role. Such a test could then be used to show that moral properties have an explanatory role. The *counterfactual test* is one such test. It claims that: "to say that z's being F is explanatorily relevant to b's being G is to say that if a had not been F then b would not have been G" (Miller 2003: 145).

Consider an example of the test in action. Imagine that a friend of yours takes up dancing lessons and you suspect that the best explanation for why he is going is that he thinks the dance instructor is attractive. A good test for whether you are right in your suspicion is to consider what would happen if the dance instructor changed. If in this case your friend stopped going to the lesson, then this is good evidence that his attraction to the dance instructor was why he was going to the dance lessons. Or consider a more serious example. We might say that if Bob had stopped smoking, then he would not have died of lung cancer. This seems like good evidence to claim that smoking killed Bob. So we have a test, the counterfactual test, which allows us to see if a property is explanatory relevant. Let us now apply it to our moral case of the soldiers bayoneting the child.

To test if the wrongness is explanatorily relevant we need to ask ourselves whether we would have judged the soldiers' action wrong if as a matter of fact the action was not wrong. An intuitive answer is "no". If their action was not wrong then one would not judge it as such. So if our counterfactual test is a good one then we are entitled to say that the wrongness *does* play a genuine explanatory role. In turn, this allows the synthetic moral realist to say that moral properties are real.

However, one might remain unimpressed by this counterfactual test. A possible concern is that the counterfactual test is meant to establish the reality of moral properties, but it works by asking us what we would believe if we removed the moral property from a situation. This looks as though the test is begging the question against the non-realist. If non-realists are right and there are *no* moral properties, then asking how our beliefs would change if there were no moral properties is not going to be a persuasive strategy. However, the synthetic moral realist has more to say that might answer the non-realists; here is where supervenience makes a return.

Recall that if our moral theory is true, then we can say that acts that bring about needless pain, suffering and death have the property of being wrong. Importantly, because of supervenience, if an action *did not* have the property of being wrong then it would not bring about needless pain, suffering and death. Armed with this extra claim we can rewrite the counterfactual test.

Imagine a case (hard as it may be) where the bayoneting of children did not involve needless pain, suffering and death: that because of a radically different set of biological laws, after the bayoneting the child laughs, jumps up and down and cries out for more. Would you judge the action as wrong? Presumably not. This means that if the counterfactual test is a good one, and if our moral theory is right, then it does seem that moral properties have a genuine explanatory role. Moral properties are real and synthetic moral realism is correct.

There is much to be said here. For instance, we might think that the counterfactual test is not as good as it first seems. We might worry that "explanation", "best explanation" and "explanatory relevance" all have importantly different meanings, or be concerned about whether we can hold our moral theory as correct while we run the counterfactual test. I shall leave the reader to pursue this further.

Synthetic realism and moral terms

Up to this point we have talked about properties. But of course we need to know from our synthetic realists how our language "links up" with moral properties. In answering this question synthetic realists split into those who think that we can give a reductive definition of our moral *terms*, and those who think that we cannot. Recall that a definition of a moral term is reductive if the definition does not include moral terms.

Railton claims that we *can* give a reductive definition – what he calls a "reforming definition" of moral terms (see e.g. Railton 2003). Does this talk of "definition" mean that his position is like Jackson's? No, because even though Railton thinks – like Jackson – that we *can* give a reductive definition of moral terms, he thinks that we establish this definition through hypothesis, speculation, trial and error; whereas Jackson thinks that we establish such a definition by giving an *a priori* conceptual analysis of our moral terms.

This distinguishes his position not only from Jackson's, but also from the Cornell realists'. The Cornell realist thinks that we cannot give any sort of definition of moral terms, since moral terms are irreducible. Moral terms stand for moral properties, *which are natural properties that cannot be reduced to any other natural properties.*

What does it mean to say that a moral property is *irreducible* (what philosophers sometimes call *sui generis*)? Consider all the actions that may be wrong: murder, breaking promises, illegally downloading music, lying, committing adultery and so on. In each case we might be able to say that because the action has a certain property(s) then it is wrong. However, is it possible to identify some property or set of properties that is in common and present in all these cases? It seems not, and if this is right then the Cornell realists are correct and we *cannot* reduce wrong to a common property or set of properties.

But then, what property makes it the case that all these things are wrong? The Cornell realist says that it is precisely *the property of being wrong*. Someone who asks "but what *is* that property?" has misunderstood. The property is wrongness. As Miller puts it in terms of moral rightness:

> We can imagine an indefinite number of ways in which actions can be morally right. [Cornell realists] think that, in *any one* example of moral rightness, the rightness can be identified in

non-moral properties. But they claim that, across *all* morally right actions, there is no one non-moral property or set of non-moral properties that all such situations have in common and to which moral rightness can be reduced.   (2003: 139)

Conclusion

If moral properties were real then we could explain a number of our common beliefs about morality. These features include such things as the belief that we can have genuine moral disagreement; the belief that we can make moral mistakes; the belief that people converge in their moral views; the intuition that there is such thing as moral progress. Moreover we can seemingly explain what it is like to experience being a moral agent.

Furthermore, if moral properties are natural properties then we can explain how we can come to interact with them and come to know about them. We can do so in the same way as we would explain how we know and interact with any natural property.

If these two points make naturalistic realism attractive then how might we identify moral properties with natural properties? The analytic realist claims that we can do this *a priori* via conceptual analysis and such an approach has been given a new lease of life through the work of Jackson.

On the other hand, the synthetic naturalists think we can identify moral properties with natural properties via *a posteriori* investigation. Railton thinks this would also involve a reduction of moral terms; Cornell realists think it would not. The plausibility of both synthetic positions turns on whether they can show that moral properties have an *explanatory role.*

One might be left thinking that although realism seems attractive, the claim that moral properties are part of the natural world is still problematic. For recall that moral properties seem to need to guide us – as Mackie argues, they seem to have a to-be-pursuedness somehow built into them. But are natural properties really like this? After all is said and done, talk of moral properties seems still to be mysterious. Of course, it was for precisely this reason that Mackie thought there were no moral properties. However, in the next chapter we shall consider a different approach. It may be true that *if* all properties that exist are natural then moral properties do not exist; but perhaps this is a good reason to think that moral properties exist but are non-natural.

THINGS TO REMEMBER

- Cornell realists think that we cannot reduce moral properties.
- It is not a challenge to Jackson's position that we cannot give the complete "moral story".
- Synthetic moral realists differ concerning how much importance they give to talk of the explanatory role of moral properties. Cornell realists think that explanatory potential is *sufficient* whereas Railton thinks it is *necessary*.
- Facts and properties are distinct although nothing turns on this distinction in this book.
- Something can be real but not mind-independent.
- Naturalists do not have to be realists.

Further reading

For a good general discussion of realism see Finlay (2007) and FitzPatrick (2009). For a good survey see Sayre-McCord (1986) and Miller (2003: chs 8, 9). Railton's and Jackson's work is tough: see Jackson (1998) and Railton (2003). A good introduction to issues about observation and explanation is Harman (1977). To help understand Cornell realism it is worth reading Bird & Tobin (2008). The *locus classicus* for Cornell realism is the tough paper written by Boyd (1988). An excellent article discussing moral explanation is Majors (2007). For a good discussion of general issues surrounding realism and analysis see Smith (1994: ch. 2). A nicely written survey and defence of realism is Shafer-Landau (2003: pt 1). For a discussion of moral naturalism see Rachels (2000), Copp (2003) and Lenman (2006). For a good general discussion of realism and anti-realism see Miller (2010).

5

Moral realism and non-naturalism

> Good is indefinable not for the reasons offered by Moore's successors, but because of the infinite difficulty of the task of apprehending a magnetic but inexhaustible reality.
>
> (Murdoch 1970: 42)

> Non-naturalism has a musty reputation, redolent of Oxbridge dons delivering the opinions of the "best and most enlightened of men" who perceive goodness just as mortals perceive yellowness ... In histories, it is noted chiefly as the theory so unacceptable that it inspired the non-cognitivists.
>
> (Shaver 2007: 283)

CHAPTER AIMS

- To explain the attractions of combining non-naturalism and moral realism.
- To outline two non-naturalist realist positions.
- To discuss the difficulties involved in demarcating naturalism from non-naturalism.

Introduction

As we discussed in the previous chapter, realism claims that:

- Moral judgements express beliefs that describe the world, and consequently moral judgements can be true or false (*cognitivism*).
- Moral judgements are sometimes true and are so in virtue of features of the world.
- The truth of moral judgements is not decided by how individuals, groups or societies think; for example, it is possible for everyone to be mistaken in their moral judgements.

The realism of this chapter differs from that of the Chapter 4 because it claims that the features that make moral claims true are not natural features but rather they are non-natural. For example, the non-naturalists would claim that if "killing is wrong" is *true* then this is because killing has the non-natural moral property of wrongness.

But why on earth would anyone in this post-Enlightenment, scientific day and age think that (a) there are moral properties and (b) these are non-natural? We shall not deal with (a), as motivations for realism have been discussed in the Chapter 4. Instead we shall discuss (b), and then consider non-naturalism in more detail via a discussion of divine command theory and Russ Shafer-Landau's moral realism.

What then is the motivation for holding that moral properties are non-natural? The issue that dominates these discussions is *normativity*.

Despite endless debates on normativity within philosophical circles there is still no clear consensus about its meaning and it remains one of the most complicated areas in philosophy. One of the many reasons for this is because normativity is present in so many branches of philosophy including the philosophy of mind, the philosophy of language, the philosophy of law, aesthetics and epistemology. It goes without saying then that the following can only be a very general feel for what philosophers mean by "normativity". For a more detailed discussion of normativity see Korsgaard (1996).

When making moral claims we use words labelled by philosophers as "normative", such as "ought" and "should". We say such things as "given that it is right to keep your promises then you *ought* to keep your promises", or "given that lying is wrong, you *should* tell the truth". When we use such words, what are we trying to convey? One thing we are trying to do is to persuade people to adopt, or not to adopt, certain behaviour. To put it in a slightly different way, such claims provide us with the ability to talk of actions being blameworthy or praiseworthy. For example, if you ought not to sell heroin to children, and you do, then you have done something wrong and you can be blamed for your action. Making moral claims directs and justifies future action.

So if realism is correct then moral properties would have to be able to guide us, justify us and provide correctness conditions for future use. Imagine how *implausible* the realist theory would seem if it claimed that moral properties exist but do not direct us, engage us or move us in any way.

In the quotation above, Murdoch (1970) states that good has a "magnetic" quality. The idea is that if good does exist then it will attract us, move us or direct us; or, as Mackie (1977) argues, moral properties would have to have "to-be-doneness" or "not-to-be-doneness" built into them. It seems then that if moral properties exist, they have to be normative.

It is of course true that natural properties can move us and can give us reason to act in one way rather than another. For example, my bike has the property of being dirty and this can give me a reason to clean it. However, some metaethicists think that such a connection is too weak to capture the requisite normativity of moral properties.

If moral properties do exist then they would justify certain actions, move us and give us reason for actions, *despite* any psychological state that we might be in. For example, if lying to a friend has the property of being wrong then this would have some guiding quality – irrespective of whether or not I wanted to lie to my friend. This contrasts with how natural properties might move us, for seemingly these properties are capable of moving us only if we have certain desires. For example, the fact that my bike has the property of being dirty *might* move me to clean it. But it might not.

Non-naturalists typically take these sorts of thoughts about normativity as good reason to believe that it is not possible to identify moral properties with *natural* properties.

> As I see it, there are genuine features of our world that remain forever outside the purview of the natural sciences. Moral facts are such features. They introduce an element of normativity that cannot be captured in the records of the natural sciences. They tell us what we *ought* to do; how we *should* behave; what is *worth* pursuing; what *reasons* we have; what is *justifiable* and what not. There is no science that can inform us of such things. (Shafer-Landau 2003: 4)

> There remains a stubborn feeling that facts about what is right or wrong, what is good or bad, and what we have reason to do have something distinctive in common, and that this common feature [normativity] is something that a natural fact could not have. (Copp 2005: 136)

> [Naturalism's] Achilles' heel (in addition to its deplorable falsehood) is that it has no room for *normativity*. There is no room, within naturalism, for right or wrong, or good or bad. (Plantinga 1998: 356)

From this very brief discussion of normativity and the issues we raised in Chapter 4 about the attractions of realism, we can show why someone might adopt non-natural realism. Realism is attractive because it captures some of our fundamental commitments in morality such as convergence, truth, disagreement, moral progress and phenomenology. But moral properties must be normative and this suggests that they are not features of the natural world. So if moral properties exist, as the realist suggests, then it seems they are non-natural. Rather than getting deeper into these issues, we shall consider the details of two non-naturalist theories.

Divine command theory: introduction and clarifications

Over the past twenty or so years divine command theory has become increasingly popular; whereas at one point it was thought that secular liberalism had crushed all life from the theory, periodicals and books are once again being populated with discussions about the possible links between God and morality.

Of course, God's role in morality is going to be non-existent to those who think that God does not exist. However, when reading this section you should put doubts about whether God exists to one side and for the sake of argument grant that he does. Moreover, even if you *do* believe in God, this does not automatically commit you to divine command theory. For example, the great theologian Thomas Aquinas favoured a *natural law theory* over a divine command theory (McDermott 1993).

Although this section concerns the commands of God this already excludes a number of highly influential theories: for example, Quinn (1978) thinks that it is what God wills rather than what he commands that is important. However, we shall stick with divine commands. And even after taking the decision to focus on divine commands, there are a large number of further issues we could discuss at length. For instance, what is the link between God's commands and what is right and wrong? Is it the case that if God commands something then this *causes* it to be right or wrong, or that God's commanding is *identical* with something being right and wrong? Or does right and wrong *supervene* on God's commands? Furthermore, for a full defence we would need to decide whether the theory is about right and wrong or good and bad. For our purposes, though, we shall stipulate divine command theory as follows:

(DCT) Something is morally right *if and only if* God commands
it. Something is wrong *if and only if* God forbids it.

Notice that for reasons we do not need to go into, the divine command theorist can argue that when people use moral language they are
still referring to God's commands *whether or not they believe in God*. So,
for instance, the existence of a morally respectable atheist is no argument against this position. For more on this point see Adams (1979).

Why is divine command theory a version of non-natural realism? And what might make it attractive?

Divine command theory appears in this chapter because it is a *non-
natural theory*. Recall that our definition of "natural" stated that what
is natural is: "the subject matter of the natural sciences and also of psychology. It may be said to include all that has existed, does exist or will
exist in time" (Moore [1903] 1993: 92). And as James Rachels says:
"Ethical naturalism is the idea that ethics can be understood in terms
of natural sciences" (2000: 75).

If something is right or wrong if and only if God commands or forbids it, then right and wrong are *not* things discoverable by the natural
sciences or psychology. God is outside the universe and independent of
the natural world. As well as being a non-natural theory, this theory is
also a *realist* theory. Realism holds that moral judgements can be true
or false, that sometimes they are true and that what makes them true is
independent from people's (or groups of people's) beliefs, judgements
or desires.

The divine command theorist holds that when we make moral judgements we are – whether we are aware of this or not – making a claim
about what God commands. Hence our moral judgements can be true
or false. Moreover, it is possible that our moral judgements *can be true*
because our moral claims may be in line with what God commands.

Finally, what we consider to be right and wrong can be completely
out of step from what God commands. It would be an odd view to think
that if *we* judge an action morally right or wrong then God would take
note and align his commands with *our* thinking on the issue. So, what is
right or wrong is independent from any society and from any culture,
at any time. If, for example, God commands that *it is right to tell the*

truth, then whatever people think, it is. Hence we can conclude that if one adopts a divine command theory one is a non-natural realist.

Why might such a view be attractive? Arguably, it is because it is very well suited to capture the source of the *normativity* of moral claims. What *justifies* the claims that morality places on us? What gives them authority over us? Divine command theory claims that God is the ultimate omniscient being and he knows better than us about ourselves, about others, about how things were, are, and will be. Moreover, God is typically thought to have sanctions in place for failing to obey him.

If, then, God commands us to do something it seems we have a reason to do it and this reason has authority. The claims that morality makes on us, such as that we should keep our promises, gain their normative status through God's legislation. These sorts of considerations might then allow divine command theory to capture the source of the normativity of morality and this in turn would make it an attractive metaethical option. However, there are a number of problems for those who support divine command theory, and we shall look at one.

If right and wrong are dependent on God's commands, then does anything go?

One popular argument against *utilitarianism* is the claim that it could morally require any action. So, for example, if in a particular instance not sacrificing children brings about worse consequences than sacrificing children, then the utilitarian would say that in this instance we are morally required to sacrifice children. The challenge continues that this sort of conclusion is wholly implausible and conflicts with what we want from any moral theory. We are left with having to either say more, or else abandon utilitarianism.

There is a similar problem for those who adopt divine command theory. Because God is sovereign he can command anything, including that we sacrifice children. It follows that it *could* be morally right to sacrifice children. But – so the problem goes – it could never be morally acceptable to do so. Hence to defend divine command theory we would need to say more. In particular, it seems we either have to abandon the very intuitive idea that some things could never be morally acceptable – such as child sacrifice – or we have to abandon divine command theory.

Someone who holds divine command theory cannot respond by saying that because child sacrifice is wrong God could not command child sacrifice. For to do so would be to claim that there are some actions, in this instance child sacrifice, that are right and wrong apart from what God commands; which of course is to abandon divine command theory, which says that it makes no sense to think of something as being right and wrong independently of God's commands.

The Euthyphro Dilemma

In his dialogue *Euthyphro*, Plato (1981) has Euthyphro saying that "holiness is what all the gods love, and unholiness is what they hate". He then famously has Socrates charge Euthyphro with the question "Do the gods love holiness because it is holy, or is it holy because they love it?" (9E1–3).

This form of argument is known as the *Euthyphro Dilemma* (although it is not actually a dilemma as it stands) and is at the heart of many of the arguments against not only divine command theories, but many other accounts as well. We can for example use the same form of argument against the view that what is right is what *society believes*: is giving to charity good because society believes it is, or does society believe it because it is good? For a fascinating discussion of the Euthyphro Dilemma as it relates to the divine command theory see Joyce (2002).

In summary, if divine command theory is successful we would have an attractive metaethical theory because it captures our realist intuitions and seems to deal well with normativity. However, this arbitrariness problem seems to create a major stumbling block to accepting the theory. In the next section we shall briefly consider how divine command theory might respond.

Responding to the arbitrariness problem

We can summarize the arbitrariness problem as the combination of three seemingly incompatible claims:

(a) Some things, such as genocide, are always morally wrong.
(b) God could command any action – including genocide.
(c) If divine command theory is true then genocide could be morally right.

Someone who wanted to defend divine command theory is then forced to give up (a) or (b). We shall now consider how plausible it would be to do so.

How might we justify giving up (a)? What seems to be justifying (a) is our moral intuition: it is our moral intuition that actions such as genocide can never be right. The idea is to hold our intuitions as correct and use them to challenge the truth of divine command theory. But intuitions themselves are *arbitrary* and untrustworthy. The particular intuitions we have arise because of things such as our class, our culture, our gender, our experiences and so on. In fact, recent work in experimental philosophy seems to suggest that a lot of the moral intuitions we hold dear are in fact based on features we would deem morally "irrelevant" and trivial (see Chapter 9 for more on this). This shows that challenging divine command theory by taking moral intuitions to be authoritative is controversial.

Although all this starts to build a case for denying (a), some people might contend that if it is even *possible* that we might have to abandon some of our most central moral beliefs then we should not adopt divine command theory. If the arbitrariness problem leads us to deny (a), then divine command theory really does have a problem. However, there may be another way of responding to the arbitrariness problem without denying (a).

We might instead accept (a) and agree that *any* action that God commanded – including such things as genocide – would be right, but maintain that there are limitations on what God could command. This response amounts to the denial of (b).

What this response is not saying is that God cannot command certain actions – such as genocide – because those actions are wrong, for this would be to claim that those actions are wrong *apart and independent* from God's will, and that would be to abandon divine command theory. Instead what is being claimed is that there is something about God's very nature that limits what he can command. Because of God's, say, justice or love, he simply *cannot* command some actions such as genocide. Wierenga puts it like this:

> the divine command theorist can even give a reason for rejecting [that God can command any action – including genocide] … namely, that *some feature of God's character*, for example, that He is essentially loving, precludes His commanding

in any possible world that a case of [e.g. genocide] be performed. (1983: 395)

Needless to say there are many things that could be said about this
approach. One might still feel that there is some circularity involved
and that appealing to God's nature is somehow a cheat. For if anything
that God could command would be right/loving/good/just and so on,
then how can rightness/love/goodness/justice and so on be a limit or
restriction on what he could command? And even if this response to
the arbitrariness challenge is successful, there are many other worries
for the divine command theory. However, we shall now turn to consider
another non-naturalist position: one that does not rely on God.

Russ Shafer-Landau: the non-naturalist's return

In his fascinating and well written book *Moral Realism* (2003) Shafer-
Landau argues that non-natural moral realism is a perfectly coherent,
defensible and attractive position. His work is part of a new and growing interest in non-naturalism (see Cuneo 2007). Using analogies with
naturalistic versions of realism and drawing arguments from other
philosophical disciplines, he defends the view that moral properties
exist and are non-natural.

Shafer-Landau argues that the best way of categorizing natural
properties and consequently non-natural properties is in terms of the
discipline of science. He writes: "Naturalism ... claims that all real
properties are those that would figure ineliminably in perfected versions of the natural and social science" (2003: 59). The idea is that if, for
example, perfected physics requires there to be quarks, then quarks are
natural properties; if perfected chemistry requires there to be sodium,
then sodium is a natural property; and so on.

If this is right, then we have a way of determining which properties are natural, and consequently which properties are non-natural:
namely, asking which properties would figure "ineliminably in a
perfected version of natural and social sciences". If Shafer-Landau is
right then whatever does so figure is natural and whatever does not is
non-natural.

Leaving aside the troubling questions about what makes something
a perfect science and what it is for a property to be ineliminable, the

question we shall consider is where moral properties would fit. Shafer-Landau argues that they would not figure ineliminably in a perfected version of natural and social science and hence that they are non-natural. This is because for Shafer-Landau ethics is *not* a natural or social science. He argues this because he thinks that what demarcates natural and social science from other disciplines is that they discover their principles and truths *a posteriori*. What makes something a science is that it precedes through experimentation, observation and empirical testing.

So if ethics is a science then these features should be central to ethics – but, according to Shafer-Landau, they are not. Rather, in ethics we come to discover moral truths *a priori*. Consider some moral questions such as "Is it right to keep promises?" or "Is genocide wrong?" In these cases, we don't discover an answer through empirical tests. If this account of the practice of ethics is correct – and we shall come back to ask whether it is – then ethics lacks the feature essential to any natural and social science. Ethics then is not a natural or social science and moral properties are not natural: or rather, moral properties – if they exist – are non-natural. Shafer-Landau writes: "Ethical nonnaturalists are those who claim that moral properties are not natural ones. This means ... that fundamental *moral truths are discoverable a priori*" (2007b: 65).

Yet what is the link between these non-natural properties and the natural properties? Can such an account respect supervenience? Is Shafer-Landau's account making our ontology more complicated than it needs to be? What makes him sure that ethical truths are discoverable *a priori*?

To answer these and other questions it is necessary to put some flesh on these bare bones. To do this we shall consider how Shafer-Landau uses the *philosophy of mind* and the discipline of *philosophy* to clarify and defend his position.

A comparison with non-reductive philosophy of mind

Shafer-Landau writes: "The sort of non-naturalism that I find appealing is one that bears a very close structural parallel to certain non-reductionist theories in the philosophy of mind" (2003: 72). What are these parallels? Shafer-Landau points to three (*ibid*.: 71–4). The first is the *multiple realizability* of mental states; the second is *property dualism*; and the third is the *anti-reductionist's accommodation of supervenience*. We shall address these in turn.

The basic idea of multiple realizability is that any mental state can be realized in an indefinite number of different ways. For example, we say that someone is in pain *irrespective* of whether they have any particular neurons or biochemistry. For instance, if an alien winced, shouted and rolled around after being kicked then we would assert that he was in pain, and we would not change our minds simply on finding out that he had special alien neurons and alien biochemistry.

Shafer-Landau thinks that this point about multiple realizability is true for moral properties. Let us consider the moral property of wrongness. We judge many actions wrong even though they have many different and distinct properties. For example, an action might cause pain or pleasure; it might be illegal or legal; public or private. Yet despite this variety we still think that all these actions can have the property of wrongness.

It follows, then, that for Shafer-Landau there is no one natural property or set of natural properties that *all* moral acts have in common and that we could identify as being identical with good, bad, right, wrong and so on. The multiple realizability of moral properties leads Shafer-Landau to claim that moral properties are irreducible, or, as philosophers like to say, *sui generis*. This is just like the discussion we had about Cornell realism in the previous chapter:

> We can imagine an *indefinite number of ways* in which actions can be morally right. [Cornell realists and now Shafer-Landau] think that, in *any one* example of moral rightness, the rightness can be identified in non-moral properties. But they claim that, across *all* morally right actions, there is no one non-moral property or set of non-moral properties that all such situations have in common and to which moral rightness can be reduced.   (Miller 2003: 39)

The second idea that Shafer-Landau develops from the philosophy of mind is the distinction between substance dualism and property dualism. When philosophers conclude that we cannot reduce mental states to physical ones, they either follow Descartes ([1641] 1996) and claim that the mind is a different substance from the body, or deny this and follow Jackson (1982) in arguing that mental properties are distinct from physical properties.

Shafer-Landau's non-naturalist moral realism takes the Jackson route. He does not think that non-natural moral properties are properties of a non-natural substance. Rather, Shafer-Landau thinks that there are non-natural moral properties that are properties of natural substances. This means he does not need to overpopulate our ontology with another substance. Shafer-Landau's theory is simpler – and perhaps, in light of this, better – than some other non-natural moral realists, such as the holders of divine command theory, who think that moral properties are non-natural properties of a non-natural substance.

The third parallel that Shafer-Landau draws with non-reductive philosophy of mind is an account of how mental states supervene on physical states. This is probably the most complex and controversial issue.

Recall that moral supervenience holds that there is no change in moral properties without change in natural properties. How can the realist respect this seeming truism? One relatively straightforward approach for the realist would be to reduce moral properties to natural properties. The realist could explain supervenience if moral properties were identical to natural ones (as Jackson claimed: see Chapter 4) because, of course, in this case to change a moral property would be one and the same thing as changing a natural property.

However, this does not help Shafer-Landau, for he thinks that moral properties cannot be reduced to natural ones: for him they are irreducible or *sui generis*. How then is he going to explain the truism that there cannot be a change in moral properties without a change in natural properties?

Shafer-Landau realizes that property dualists in the philosophy of mind will also have had to deal with this issue, for it seems to be true that we cannot change someone's *mental* state without changing some physical state – although this is perhaps less obvious in the mental case than in the moral one. So he looks to see what answers the property dualists in the philosophy of mind give to the problem of accounting for supervenience.

The account that Shafer-Landau uses is the claim that mental states are exhaustively constituted by the physical states but that they cannot be reduced to those physical states. His account uses the idea that constitution is not the same as identity. He says:

> According to the sort of ethical non-naturalism that I favour, a moral fact supervenes on a particular concatenation of descriptive facts just because these facts *realize* the moral property in question. Moral facts [supervene on] descriptive ones because moral properties are always realized exclusively by descriptive ones. (2003: 77)

This needs more discussion than I can give here (see Mabrito 2005; Ridge 2007) but we can illustrate the difference between constitution and identity by using a well-known example.

Imagine a clay statue. We might be tempted to say that the property of being a statue supervenes on the property of being clay, because we cannot make a change to the statue without making some change to the clay. For example, we cannot move the arm of the statue without making some change to the clay.

We think this is true because the clay – and the clay alone – constitutes the statue. Yet – and this is the crucial point – we do not want to say that the statue is *identical* to the clay. This is because we think that if two things are identical they will share the same properties, yet the clay has some properties that are *not* shared with the statue: for example, clay has the property of remaining clay even when you hit it with a big hammer, whereas the statue does not have the property of remaining a statue when you do the same. Because of this difference in properties, we can say that the statue and the clay are *not* identical, while also holding that the clay exhaustively constitutes the statue and consequently that supervenience is respected.

This is similar to Shafer-Landau's argument in the moral case. Because there is a difference between natural and moral properties, we can say they are not identical; however, natural properties exhaustively constitute moral properties and consequently the moral properties supervene on the natural properties. A discussion about how convincing this is would take us too far into metaphysics but it is certainly an interesting suggestion and one that is worthy of further research.

In summary, we can see that by borrowing from non-reductive accounts in the philosophy of mind, Shafer-Landau thinks he can reject the identification of moral properties with natural ones; he thinks his non-natural account is not ontologically extravagant because he does not need a new non-natural *substance*; and he thinks he can explain supervenience without endorsing the reduction of moral properties to natural ones.

However, Shafer-Landau's position is now starting to sound very much like Cornell realism, the view that moral properties are irreducible and multiply realizable, and supervene on natural properties. It seems that unless there is a way of separating Cornell realism and Shafer-Landau's account then Shafer-Landau is a naturalist moral realist, or Cornell realists are *non-naturalists,* after all.

A comparison with philosophy

Recall that for Shafer-Landau the way to show that moral properties are *non*-natural is epistemological. Therefore the way to distance himself from Cornell realism is to address the question: "How do we come to know about ethical truths?" If the answer is "primarily through *empirical* investigation" then this means that ethics *is* like a natural science and his position would be just like Cornell realism.

If, on the other hand, ethics progresses through *a priori* investigation then ethics is not like a natural or social science and moral properties are non-natural. His account could then be shown to be distinct from naturalistic versions of moral realism. Shafer-Landau supports this latter option via a comparison with the discipline of philosophy. In particular he argues that philosophy works through *a priori* investigation; ethics is part of the discipline of philosophy, and consequently it works through *a priori* investigation. Therefore ethics is not a science and moral properties are non-natural. We shall now consider this in a little more detail.

Consider how philosophers go about studying philosophy. For example, imagine that a metaphysician you know is applying for a research grant to study universals, tropes and possible worlds. When she is costing her research bid, does she need to allocate money to buy new lab equipment, lab coats, and safety apparatus? No! As philosophers, our beliefs about whether there are possible worlds, universals, free will, God and so on are not dependent on getting the right results in empirical tests. Arguably, philosophy is not an empirical discipline but an *a priori* one.

For this reason, Shafer-Landau thinks that philosophy is *not* a natural or social science. For recall that natural and social sciences are identified by an *a posteriori* method. But if this is true, then *no* subdiscipline of philosophy will be a natural or social science.

Ethics is a subdiscipline of philosophy, which means that it too is not a natural or social science. Hence Shafer-Landau concludes that if moral properties exist they must be non-natural. This in turn means Shafer-Landau can distance himself from the synthetic realists discussed in the previous chapter, for they *did* think that ethics is best thought of as a science. Richard Boyd, a Cornell realist, writes: "I should say something about how the claim that the nature of the constituents of moral goodness is an empirical matter should be understood. I mean the analogy between moral inquiry and scientific inquiry to be taken *very* seriously" (1988: 122).

Given these points, Shafer-Landau concludes:

> [Cornell realism] is a picture which I, counting myself a non-naturalist, accept in all essentials. The only difference between [us] lies in whether or not one is willing to count moral properties as natural ones. And, as far as I can tell, the only importance in the classification at this stage is methodological and epistemological. The importance, to be specific, lies in whether we are willing to count ethics as a kind of science, and whether we believe that we can discover ethical truths in just the same way that natural and social scientists discover truths in their respective disciplines [he of course does not].   (2003: 64)

Is Shafer-Landau's characterization of philosophy right? After all, as we noted in the section on divine command theory there has been a growing interest in experimental philosophy, which *does* run experiments and empirical tests. Moreover, we might think that ethics is philosophical for reasons other than epistemological or methodological ones. Or we might take a different tack, arguing that there are reasons to think that ethics progresses *a posteriori* and that this gives us reason to think that when we are doing ethics we are not doing philosophy.

To conclude, Shafer-Landau attempts to defend a version of non-natural realism. He uses the fact that ethics is a subdiscipline of philosophy to argue that moral properties are non-natural. He thinks that his non-naturalism is not as odd as we may think and that an analogy with reductive philosophy of mind allows him to address the most common worries levelled at moral non-natural realists. The overall plausibility of such an account remains to be seen. What is clear is that Shafer-Landau is one of a new movement of metaethicists arguing for non-naturalism as a genuine option.

Conclusion

Realism is attractive because it can capture many features of morality. Non-naturalism is an increasingly popular theory and its attraction lies in the belief that ethics is not a science and that the normativity of moral properties *cannot* be reduced to natural properties.

New-wave non-naturalists such as Shafer-Landau have again reinvigorated the debate and have shown how old worries – for example, about the strangeness of non-natural substances and how the non-natural can supervene on the natural – are not as devastating as we might first have thought.

Despite all this, a number of metaethicists would claim that we have been far too hasty in accepting realism. They suggest that we can capture any feature of morality the realist cares to name while at the same time rejecting realism. In the next chapter we shall consider one such position: *quasi-realism*.

THINGS TO REMEMBER

- It is possible to be a non-naturalist and not be a theist.
- It is possible to be a theist, but not a divine command theorist.
- It is possible to be a property dualist, but not a substance dualist.
- The divine command theorist can argue that when people use moral language they are referring to God's commands whether or not they believe in God.
- Our discussion regarding the divine command theory is not about how we might come to know about God's commands, or how we might live if the divine command theory is correct.
- It is possible to be a non-naturalist without being a moral realist.

Further reading

For Shafer-Landau's account see Shafer-Landau (2003: ch. 3; 2007a: ch. 16). For a discussion of normativity see Korsgaard (1996) and Finlay (2010), and on divine command theory see Quinn (2000), Joyce (2002) and Murphy (2008). For a summary of non-reductive accounts in the philosophy of mind see Lowe (2000: chs 2, 3). See Cuneo (2007) and FitzPatrick (2009) for a summary of realist accounts. For an interesting paper looking at the parallels between theological and moral realism see Shafer-Landau (2007c). For a good general discussion of what is real, natural and non-natural see McNaughton (1988).

6

Quasi-realism

Some philosophers like to call themselves realists, and some like to call themselves anti-realists. An increasing number, I suspect, wish to turn their backs on the whole issue.   (Blackburn 2007: 47)

CHAPTER AIMS

- To explain the Frege–Geach problem.
- To explain quasi-realism and how it can respond to the Frege–Geach problem.
- To pose a number of problems for quasi-realism.
- To describe some problems with trying to demarcate cognitivism from non-cognitivism.

Introduction

Quasi-realism starts from a non-cognitivist position and it may be easier to understand it if we first consider why non-cognitivism developed as it did. Non-cognitivism grew in popularity after the publication of Moore's *Principia Ethica* in 1903. Although non-cognitivists believe that the truth in Moore's work is that moral terms cannot be defined, they also think that Moore was wrong to reach for non-natural properties as an explanation for this. Instead, the non-cognitivist rejects realism and claims that moral judgements express not *beliefs* but rather *non-cognitive states*. Part of the attraction of non-cognitivism is that it seems to respect the insights of Moore's work without resorting to non-naturalism, which is thought to be ontologically problematic. However, something was looming on the horizon that would take the wind out of the non-cognitivist's sails and would change the metaethical landscape, a problem that some philosophers believe has left non-cognitivism dead in the water: the Frege–Geach problem.

The Frege–Geach problem

It is a shame that the Frege–Geach problem can seem rather complex at first sight because the fundamental issue is relatively straightforward. It is understandable, however, how this impression arises, for the Frege–Geach problem has generated some of the most obscure and technical literature in metaethics. The goal of this section is to outline clearly and simply the Frege–Geach problem.

Before launching into the Frege–Geach problem, we need first to refresh our memories as to what the non-cognitivist believes. This is that when we *make* a moral judgement we express non-cognitive states and the type of non-cognitive state we opt for will demarcate the type of non-cognitivist we are: for instance, Ayer ([1936] 1974) claimed that it was emotions that are expressed; Hare (1952) claimed that it was prescriptions; and more recently Gibbard (1990) has claimed we express states of norm-acceptance. Furthermore, even though the non-cognitivists believe that moral judgements express non-cognitive states, they do not think that this is evident from how we speak. *The non-cognitivist and cognitivist both aim to leave everyday moral language as it is.*

The Frege–Geach problem

The Frege–Geach problem was first stated by Peter Geach (1958, 1960, 1965) when he challenged non-cognitivism by pointing out that (i) the meaning of moral terms do not vary across asserted and unasserted contexts; and (ii) in our moral language the non-cognitivist *is* committed to the meaning varying across asserted and unasserted contexts. Geach thinks that these ideas are implicit in Frege's treatment of "not" (hence *Frege–Geach*). For an excellent overview of the Frege–Geach problem see Schroeder (2008).

In a nutshell the Frege–Geach problem is that if non-cognitivism is true then the *meaning* of moral claims varies depending on whether they are asserted or not. Yet when we reflect on our moral practice, we do not think that the meaning of moral claims varies in this way. Therefore either non-cognitivism is wrong or we are mistaken in our belief about how moral language works. Faced with this alternative, the simplest and most attractive choice might seem to be to reject non-cognitivism, for we might think that we have some authority on how our own moral language works. We shall now put some more detail into this argument, starting with the claim that for the non-cognitivist the meaning of a moral claim changes depending on whether it is asserted or unasserted.

The distinction between asserting a moral claim or not is that we are asserting a moral claim if we are *actually* making a moral judgement; for example, saying "killing is wrong" is asserting that killing is wrong. In contrast, there are a number of ways in which we can use moral claims without actually asserting them: for example, we can use them in conditionals (i.e. if … then …) or in disjunctions (i.e. "or"), we can report what people believe, or use them in questions. If I say "*If* child sacrifice is wrong, *then* Abraham was wrong to attempt to sacrifice Isaac", this is a conditional in which I am *not* asserting that child sacrifice is wrong. If I say "Child sacrifice is wrong *or* lying is wrong" this is a *disjunction* and I am not asserting that child sacrifice is wrong. Or, if I say "Neil believes that killing is wrong", I am reporting what Neil believes; I am not asserting that killing is wrong. Finally, if I ask "*Is* child sacrifice wrong?" this is a question, and I am not actually asserting that child sacrifice is wrong.

If non-cognitivism is right then when we assert a moral claim we are expressing a non-cognitive state, whereas if we are *not* asserting a moral claim we are *not* expressing a non-cognitive state: so if I assert "Child sacrifice is wrong", I am expressing a non-cognitive state, whereas if I say "*If* child sacrifice is wrong, *then* Abraham was wrong to attempt to sacrifice Isaac", then – given that I am not asserting that child sacrifice is wrong – I am *not* expressing a non-cognitive state.

The key things to remember thus far are these: first, there are many devices in our language – such as conditionals, disjunctions and questions – that allow us to use moral claims without asserting them. Second, according to the non-cognitivist a speaker only expresses a non-cognitive state if a moral claim is asserted.

The problem is brought into sharp focus when we add a third claim that according to the non-cognitivist the *meaning* of a claim varies depending on whether or not we are expressing a non-cognitive state. According to the non-cognitivist, if we make a moral claim and express a non-cognitive state then this will have a different meaning from a case in which we make the same claim and do not express a non-cognitive state. Given that in our moral talk we sometimes assert moral claims, and sometimes use moral claims without asserting them, then it appears that if non-cognitivists are right the meanings of moral claims are not fixed. This is because in some instances we express non-cognitive states and in some we do not. An example will clarify this point: if we assert "Killing is wrong", then it will have a non-cognitive meaning, whereas if we say, "*If* killing is wrong, *then* soldiers should not kill", then – because "killing is wrong" is *not* asserted – "killing is wrong" in this conditional will have a different meaning.

This sounds rather abstract, so why should the non-cognitivist lose sleep over this? The answer is because it seems highly counter-intuitive to think that meaning fluctuates in this sort of way. Consider another example to illustrate this. If I were to ask "Do you think killing is wrong?", it seems perfectly satisfactory for you to answer "Yes, killing is wrong". Yet for the non-cognitivist this does *not* count as an answer, because when I asked *whether* killing is wrong, I was not asserting that killing *is* wrong. But when you answered "Yes, killing *is* wrong" then you were asserting that "Killing is wrong". So, given that the non-cognitivist thinks the meaning of a moral claim will change depending on whether it is asserted or not, the answer means something different from what is being asked, and "Yes, killing is wrong" is not an answer to the question! If non-cognitivism is right, then the answer "Killing is wrong" is as far-off an answer to the question "Is killing wrong?" as, say, "Train station", "Pluto", or "Carbuncle". It is clear why this is a problem for non-cognitivists: it seems to fly in the face of common sense.

Let us consider another example to illustrate the Frege–Geach problem, one in which we mix asserted and unasserted moral claims via the conditional rather than a question. Consider the conditional in *modus ponens*:

1. *A*
2. If *A* then *B*

Therefore,

3. *B*.

If anything is valid, then this is. Moreover, logicians tell us that logic is *topic-neutral*, which means that this form of argument will remain valid whatever we care to substitute for *A* and *B*. For example, if we substitute "cats are cute", "if cats are cute then they should be stroked" and therefore, "cats should be stroked", we have a valid argument. Key to appreciating the problem for non-cognitivists is that A in (1) is *asserted*, whereas – because of the conditional – A in (2) is *unasserted*.

So this means that if we substitute A for a *moral* claim then – because for the non-cognitivist moral claims change meaning depending on whether they are asserted or not – A will mean one thing in (1) and something different in (2). This in turn means that for non-cognitivists, if we use moral claims in the form of *modus ponens*, then the argument is *invalid*. This is perhaps even more counter-intuitive than the last example. To put this point in a different way: non-cognitivists seem committed to denying that *modus ponens* is topic-neutral. To illustrate this problem, consider an argument that has the *modus ponens* form and has morality as its subject:

4. Torture is wrong.
5. If torture is wrong, then the government ordering soldiers to torture is wrong.

Therefore,

6. The government ordering soldiers to torture is wrong.

This looks valid, but for the non-cognitivist it is not. In (4) we have asserted that "torture is wrong" but in (5) "torture is wrong" is *not* asserted. Consequently the non-cognitivist will hold that in (4) we are expressing a non-cognitive state whereas in (5) we are not. Therefore "torture is wrong" has a different meaning in each of (4) and (5). But if there is a difference in meaning then the argument cannot be valid, as this mixing of meanings implies that there is an informal fallacy being committed: the *fallacy of equivocation*. Here is another argument that is invalid because it commits this fallacy:

7. My hand is on this mouse.
8. If your hand is on a mouse then it squeaks.

Therefore,

9. This mouse squeaks.

This argument is invalid because it equivocates on the meaning of the terms in the argument; in this case, "mouse" refers to a computer part in (7) but an animal in (8).

The Frege–Geach problem shows that for the non-cognitivist, using morality as the subject of *modus ponens* is to commit the *fallacy of equivocation*. Hence we have illustrated how easy it is to mix assertions with non-assertions. In our simple examples we used a question and a conditional. We have claimed that this mixing of contexts means that the non-cognitivist is committed to the meaning of moral claims being unstable, yet we thought that this was counter-intuitive. So the non-cognitivist has a problem because we do not make a special case out of our moral language by saying, for example, that *modus ponens* is valid except when the subject is morality.

At this stage it is worth pre-empting a common mistake. Students often think that the non-cognitivist is easily able to respond to this challenge of the modus ponens by showing that (4)–(6) is valid by rewriting it like this:

10. Boo! Torture.
11. If Boo! Torture, then Boo! government ordering soldiers to torture.

Therefore,

12. Boo! Government ordering soldiers to torture.

Surely, they claim, we have preserved the validity without giving up anything essential to non-cognitivism. The problem is that this "solution" misses the point. In (10) we are *expressing* Boo! to torture and thus it has one meaning. But (11) is *not* expressing Boo! to torture: (11) is still a conditional and is describing a possible situation in which we might express Boo! to torture. Thus, given that the non-cognitivist is committed to the meaning of moral claims being a function of whether they are asserted or not, "Boo! to torture" has different meanings in (10) and (11). This rewrite to try and help the non-cognitivist has not helped, and the argument remains invalid because it still commits the fallacy of equivocation. The Frege–Geach problem remains a problem.

To finish this section, let us consider why there is no Frege–Geach problem for the cognitivist (although Gibbard [2003] disagrees). The cognitivist can argue that moral *modus ponens* is valid in the same way as non-moral *modus ponens*. For the cognitivist, what a claim describes does not change depending on whether it is asserted or not. If we say "torture is wrong" then we are describing the world as being a certain way; if we say "if torture is wrong, then what Bill did was wrong" then the claim "torture is wrong", is describing an identical but possible state of affairs.

For the cognitivist the meaning of a moral claim is dependent on its description. It follows then that because moral claims do not describe something different, or cease to be descriptions, whether or not they are asserted, the meaning of moral claims does not change meaning. This means that there is no Frege–Geach problem for the cognitivist. For cognitivism the same proposition is first asserted, then not asserted. The problem for non-cognitivism is that there is no attitudinal analogue for the proposition. We may then be led to conclude that non-cognitivism should be rejected. However, quasi-realists think that this would be too hasty.

Quasi-realism

One of the main proponents of quasi-realism is Simon Blackburn and for brevity we shall focus on his work. He has written extensively on the position and his work is complex, rich and well written. And because he sees quasi-realism as an ongoing explanatory story, his views have continued to change (in fact, he is now unhappy with the label "non-cognitivist" but we shall leave that for now). We shall be primarily dealing with his earlier work, *Spreading the Word* (1984), which will give us a flavour of his overall project.

Blackburn makes it clear that quasi-realism is not another position but an explanatory programme. The task he sets himself is explaining how it is that we have arrived at a situation where our moral practice *appears* to be realist when in fact realism is false. Rosen puts it like this: "Blackburn's strategy is to construct a position which embraces all of the pregnant rhetoric of realism without qualification or reservation or devious reinterpretation of the language, but which is nonetheless recognizably antirealist in spirit" (1998: 386).

This, of course, is why Blackburn calls the explanatory programme quasi-realism: it resembles or simulates realism without actually being realism. Blackburn sets out to explain the realist features of our moral practice from the starting point of non-cognitivism. So, what are these features of our moral practice? Blackburn lists a few:

> [W]hether the anti-realist can make sense of thoughts like "I would like to know whether bullfighting is wrong," or "I believe that bullfighting is wrong, but I might be wrong about that," or "Bullfighting would be wrong whatever I or anyone else thought about it" – *claims asserting our concern to get things right, our fallibility, and some independence of the ethical from what we actually feel.*   (1993: 4, emphasis added)

Blackburn argues that quasi-realism is capable of explaining how the non-cognitivist can earn the right to talk in this way. In fact, Blackburn argues that not only can quasi-realism do this but it can do it in a way that makes non-cognitivism more attractive than realism. Thus quasi-realism is not just an explanatory programme; it also justifies non-cognitivism over realism.

To sum up, Blackburn is a non-cognitivist; he thinks that moral judgements express non-cognitive states. However, unlike earlier non-cognitivists such as Ayer, he is not happy to leave it at that. Blackburn argues that we need to pay more respect to the realist-seeming nature of our moral practice. Quasi-realism is his name for the attempt to explain the realist-seeming nature of our moral practice even though realism is false. The quasi-realist is "a person who, starting from a recognizably anti-realist position, finds himself progressively able to mimic the intellectual practices supposedly definitive of realism" (Blackburn 1993: 15). We shall consider how plausible this explanatory programme is, starting with the Frege–Geach problem.

Blackburn and the Frege–Geach problem

Given what we have said in the section above, Blackburn needs a response to the Frege–Geach problem. This is one particular area in which Blackburn keeps refining his responses (e.g. Blackburn 1984, 1993, 1998). We shall consider his first attempt, which he now rejects. Key to understanding Blackburn's response is the notion of sensibility.

Someone's sensibility is the set of dispositions that ground how they will react to certain situations. A sensibility might include, for example, the disposition to get angry at injustice, the disposition to cry at cruelty or the disposition to smile at acts of charity. Each one of us has our own sensibility.

It seems that we approve of some sensibilities over others; that is, we approve of certain combinations of dispositions over other combinations. In particular, we prefer sensibilities that lead people to be *consistent* in how they react to situations. We think more of people who have consistent views, and we feel that we can approve and endorse such sensibilities.

Contrast this with those sensibilities that lead people to act in inconsistent ways. We would think that they had what Blackburn calls "a fractured sensibility". Blackburn will use this approval of some sensibilities, and disapproval of others, as a way of showing how the Frege–Geach problem can be solved, at least in the *modus ponens* case.

Consider again our *modus ponens* argument:

4. Torture is wrong.
5. If torture is wrong, then the government ordering soldiers to torture is wrong.

Therefore,

6. The government ordering soldiers to torture is wrong.

What Blackburn needs is a way of explaining why if someone accepted (4) and (5) they rationally ought to accept (6); or, to put it another way, why someone who accepts (4) and (5) would resist denying (6). Importantly, Blackburn must give this explanation as a non-cognitivist; that is, without talking in terms of validity and truth.

To see how he goes about doing this we must first think about (4)–(6) in terms of non-cognitive attitudes – let us say approval and disapproval. Premise (4) is pretty simple – we can think of this as having the attitude of disapproval towards torture. What about the conditional (5)?

This is where the talk of sensibility comes in. Blackburn's proposal is that (5) is read as an attitude towards someone's *moral sensibility*: that is, that the conditional "if torture is wrong, then the government ordering soldiers to torture is wrong" is a way of expressing disapproval towards those people who have the sensibility that *combines* disapproval of torture with a lack of disapproval of the government ordering soldiers to torture.

The introduction of approval and disapproval towards sensibility then gives Blackburn an account of why we cannot deny (6) if we accept (4) and (5), an account that does not rely on talk of truth and validity.

Accepting (4) would be to disapprove of torture. Accepting (5) would be to disapprove of those people who both disapprove of torture *and* lack disapproval of the government ordering soldiers to torture.

Yet if we disapprove of those people who disapprove of torture but who also lack disapproval of the government ordering soldiers to torture, then, if we are to be consistent, we ourselves should disapprove of government ordering soldiers to torture. It follows then that we rationally ought to accept (6). We would be inconsistent, having a fractured sensibility, if we disapproved of torture (4), disapproved of those people who disapprove of torture but who lack disapproval of ordering soldiers to torture (5) but ourselves lacked the disapproval of the government ordering soldiers to torture – that is, if we denied (6). It seems then that here is a way of explaining why (6) follows from (4) and (5), and why we feel there has been a mistake in a case where (4) and (5) are accepted but (6) denied.

So for Blackburn, in cases of moral *modus ponens*, the validity is not really validity as we would traditionally conceive it but rather is about holding a consistent, or non-fractured, moral sensibility.

As Blackburn would put it, concerning someone holding (4) disapproval of torture and (5) disapproval of those who disapprove of torture and lack disapproval of the government ordering soldiers to torture: "Anyone holding this pair *must* hold the consequential disapproval: he is committed to disapproving of [the government ordering soldiers to torture], for if he does not his *attitudes clash*. He has a *fractured sensibility* which cannot itself be an object of approval." (1984: 195, emphasis added).

The key thing to remember is that by using the idea that we can approve or disapprove of people's sensibilities, we can show why we think *modus ponens* with the subject of morality is valid, when in fact it is not. The non-cognitivist position then starts to seem less counterintuitive. Blackburn has started to respond to the Frege–Geach problem.

There is a lot to ask about this approach: for instance, in what sense can something be a consequential disapproval? What type of mistake is a fractured sensibility? How can this approach help in other instances where there is a mix of asserted and unasserted contexts – such as our question "is killing wrong"?

In the end Blackburn (1998) has given up this sort of approach and with it talk of "fractured sensibilities". However, we shall leave this to one side, as Blackburn has not yet covered the "quasi-realist" part of the theory. That is, although we have shown how the non-cognitivist might be able to respond to this manifestation of the Frege–Geach problem, we have not heard a reason as to why our language has developed to suggest that moral *modus ponens* is valid; and, in general, why our language has developed in a way that suggests realism is true, despite its falsity.

Blackburn uses a thought experiment to show why we might arrive at realism even though non-cognitivism is true. He starts by asking us to imagine that our moral language is purely non-cognitivist and does *not* contain any moral predicates. In this language we would not say "killing is wrong", or "giving to charity is right". Rather, such a language "might contain a 'hooray!' operator and a 'boo!' operator (H!, B!) which attach to the descriptions of things to result in expressions of attitude. H! (the playing of Tottenham Hotspur) would express the attitude towards the playing" (1984: 193). However, from this starting-point Blackburn thinks that if this purely expressivist language is ever going to be any use in our *moral* practice at all, it would have to "*become* an instrument of serious reflective, evaluative practice, able to express concern for improvements, clashes, implications, and coherence of attitudes" (*ibid.*: 195).

Thus Blackburn's suggestion is that for us to be able to use a purely expressivist language as a moral language, it would have to develop moral predicates; and furthermore, it would have to evolve to have the features that we typically associate with realism. So, to put it another way, a purely expressive language would have to evolve to have the surface features of realism. As Blackburn says, starting from a purely non-cognitivist language, we would have to:

> invent a predicate answering to the attitudes, and treat commitments *as if they were judgements*, and then use all the natural devices for debating truth. If this is right, then our use of [unasserted] contexts does not prove that an expressive theory of morality is wrong; it merely proves us to have adopted a form of expression adequate to our needs. (*Ibid.*)

Blackburn's explanation is apparently pragmatic. For us to *do* what we want with our moral language it has to be realist.

In this section we have suggested how Blackburn thinks that by using the notion of sensibilities he can respond to the Frege–Geach problem. Moreover, Blackburn argues that our moral language has developed from non-cognitivism to have the outward appearance of realism because the realist language is needed in order for moral language to function properly. We shall now consider a number of issues regarding quasi-realism.

Three reasons to reject realism

Quasi-realists say that realism is false, but that they can explain why – when considering our moral practice – we come to think that realism is true. But surely we are missing a trick. The obvious way of explaining why realism is true is that – it is!

Quasi-realists are fully aware of such a worry and give reasons for rejecting realism. Blackburn has a number, but we shall consider just three: economy, practicality and supervenience. I shall quickly mention the first two, and spend a little longer on the third.

Blackburn's first argument against realism is economy. The basic idea here is that non-cognitivism is more economical than realism in terms of what exists and epistemology. The non-cognitivist account requires the natural world and people's non-cognitive states. Realism is rather more "expensive" in terms of what exists, and the account of knowledge for it requires moral properties and some account of how we come to know about these moral properties. If we grant for the sake of argument that the best explanations are the most economical, then non-cognitivism is preferable to realism.

The second argument relates to issues in moral psychology and if you read Chapter 8 you will have a better appreciation of the issue. However, we can outline the basic idea here. Blackburn holds the Humean account of motivation, which is a combination of two ideas. First, when someone is motivated then this is always because of the presence of a belief and an appropriately related desire. The second component is that beliefs cannot entail desires because beliefs and desires are fundamentally distinct mental states.

As well as the Humean account, Blackburn accepts *motivational internalism*. This is roughly the idea that if we make a moral judgement then we shall necessarily be motivated by that judgement. Again, grant this for the sake of argument. Internalism is also discussed in more detail in Chapter 8.

We are now ready to see how Blackburn's second argument against realism works. If internalism is true then moral judgements *necessarily* motivate. If the Humean account is correct then motivation necessarily requires desires and furthermore *beliefs cannot entail desires*. What seems to follow from this is that *moral judgements cannot be beliefs*, because if they were beliefs then desires might not be present when we make moral judgements. But that would mean that motivation might not follow from the judgement. Yet this is conceptually impossible if internalism is correct. Therefore, moral judgements cannot be beliefs. Cognitivism is false, and with it, so is realism.

In contrast, if, as the non-cognitivist would say, moral judgements are expressions of desires (or other non-cognitive states), then necessarily desires will be present when we make a moral judgement and on making a moral judgement we shall necessarily be motivated to act. Thus non-cognitivism seems preferable to cognitivism, given the truth of the Humean account of motivation and motivational internalism.

Finally, let us consider the "supervenience" argument. Recall that moral supervenience is the claim that if two things have identical natural properties then they will necessarily have the same moral properties. As Blackburn says: "It seems *conceptually* impossible to suppose if two things are identical in every other respect one is better than the other. Such a difference could *only* arise if there were other differences between them" (1984: 183).

If, for example, when presented with two abortion cases we claimed that one was wrong and the other right, then unless we are going to be accused of conceptual confusion we need to be able to identify some difference between them. Perhaps in one case we think that the foetus's nervous system is fully developed, whereas it is not in the other. Blackburn's question is how the realist can respect moral supervenience.

One approach for the realist would be to define moral terms in natural terms and claim that moral properties are identical with natural ones. The realist could explain supervenience if this was the case because then a change in a moral property would be the same as a change in a natural property. It would not make sense to say that two things were identical in their natural properties but differed in their moral properties if moral properties were just natural properties.

However, Blackburn thinks this realist way of responding to supervenience would be far too powerful because the realist shouldn't be committed to the claim that in *any* possible world a certain natural property(s) would guarantee as a matter of conceptual or logical necessity a moral property being present. He thinks it is implausible that we can "read off" that a moral property is present by simply fully understanding the natural property (or properties). This is because what allows us to claim that a certain moral property is present is the theory we have. It is only with our moral theory in place that we can say that given a natural property then the moral property is present. For instance, if our theory says that pain is wrong, then when pain occurs we can say it is wrong. And it is *not* the case that merely understanding the natural properties – in isolation from a theory – means that we know the moral properties have to be present. We cannot simply think about pain, independent of our moral theory, and come to the conclusion that it is wrong. As Blackburn says:

> [I]t does not seem a matter of conceptual or logical necessity that any given total natural state of a thing gives it some particular moral quality. For to tell which moral quality results from a given natural state means using *standards whose correctness cannot be shown by conceptual means alone*. It means *moralizing* and bad people moralize badly, but need not be confused. (*Ibid.*: 184, emphasis added)

With these parts in place, we can put Blackburn's challenge to the realist: explain the relationship between moral and natural properties such that it is "*conceptually* impossible to suppose that if two things are identical in natural properties one is better than the other" (*ibid.*: 183). But do not do this by using a necessary link between moral and natural properties that is conceptual or logical. Blackburn thinks that such a task is impossible. "Supervenience then becomes a mysterious fact, and one which [the realist] will have no explanation of (or right to rely upon)" (*ibid.*: 185).

Of course, this would only show quasi-realism to be in a better position if quasi-realism *can* explain supervenience. Blackburn thinks it can:

> supervenience can be explained in terms of the constraints upon [expressing]. Our purpose in [expressing] value predicates may demand that we respect supervenience. If we allowed ourselves a system (shmoralizing) which was like

ordinary evaluative practice, but subject to *no* such [super-venience] constraint, then it would allow us to treat natural identical cases in morally different ways. This could be good shmoralizing. But that would *unfit shmoralizing from being any kind of guide to practical decision-making.*

(*Ibid.*: 186, emphasis added)

Blackburn thinks that any moral system that does not respect super-venience would be useless as a guide to practical decision-making. Yet, at root, a moral practice needs to be a guide to practical decision-making, so any moral practice would need – by virtue of being a moral practice – to respect supervenience. This means that if non-cognitivism is true then we would *have* to evolve to incorporate supervenience into our morality. Blackburn's explanation of supervenience is *pragmatic*. If our moral practice does not respect supervenience, then morality will not be fit for purpose.

Given these three arguments – economy, practicality and superveni-ence – Blackburn thinks we should accept quasi-realism over realism. There are many things which can, and have, been said about these argu-ments (see Further Reading below). I shall leave the reader to think about these issues further. In the final section, we shall consider a chal-lenge to quasi-realism. This will lead us into asking a more general question about cognitivism and non-cognitivism.

What, if anything, is the defining feature of non-cognitivism?

Taking into account the discussion in this chapter and in Chapter 3, when a metaethicist says "I'm a non-cognitivist", what are they tell-ing us? Perhaps they are simply using this as shorthand for: "Don't lump me in with those realists". But if we were to push the issue fur-ther, what would they identify as those views which pick *them* out as non-cognitivists?

One starting-point might be that when we make moral judgements we *express* something, but this looks unhelpful, given its generality. Perhaps we shall make some progress if we ask *what* is expressed. Yet non-cognitivists such as Stevenson (1944), Hare (1952), Ayer ([1936] 1974), Blackburn (1984) and Gibbard (1990) will give *different* answers, so this might be too crude a way of demarcating non-cognitivism from cognitivism. However, there might be something in it, for these philosophers would agree that whatever moral judgements do express, it is not a *belief*.

Perhaps we have a way of identifying a non-cognitivist position: a non-cognitivist is someone who thinks that moral judgements do not express beliefs. This sounds fair, but what does it mean? Can we say anything else about what would distinguish a moral judgement that expressed a belief from one that expressed a non-belief state? One possible way to answer this is by recalling that if moral judgements *do* express beliefs then they could be true or false. Thus one way of identifying non-cognitivism is to consider further the idea that moral judgements are *not* truth-apt.

Returning to quasi-realism, recall that it is successful in as far as it can explain the surface features of our moral discourse. We mentioned a number of these features above: fallibility; the ability to come to know something is right or wrong; and talk of moral properties. Yet there is one crucial thing we have not mentioned. In our moral practice we believe that moral judgements can be truth-apt: for example, when we say that it is morally wrong that some people in the world still do not have access to sanitation, electricity and water, we think that this claim is either true or false. So quasi-realism needs to show how moral judgements can be truth-apt, even though non-cognitivism is correct.

The quasi-realist agrees that this needs to be explained and moreover that the explanation must not involve talk of beliefs. This is because if truth-aptness simply entailed belief then in securing truth-aptness the quasi-realist would have shown cognitivism to be correct. Luckily for the quasi-realist, there is a theory of truth-aptness that does not require talk of belief at all. This position is the minimalist account of truth-aptness (note that this is not minimalism about truth: see Chapter 10; Engel 2002).

Roughly put, minimalism about truth-aptness holds that if the central claims of a practice *seem* truth-apt, then they are. Most importantly, in this case there is no further question to be asked about whether the claims express beliefs. What would a practice have to have in order for the minimalist to argue its central claims are truth-apt? The language in the practice would have to be disciplined (there are acknowledged standards for the proper and improper use) and the language would have to have the right sort of syntactic features (capable of being used in conditionals [if … then …], negations [not …], conjunctions [… and …] and disjunctions [… or …] and so on).

If we now turn to consider moral practice, the minimalist account allows us to say that moral judgements *are* truth-apt. For moral practice does have acknowledged appropriate and inappropriate standards of use. There are times when it is suitable to claim things such as "integrity is right" or "killing is wrong", and times when it is not. Furthermore, we can use moral claims with conditionals, negations, conjunctions and disjunctions and so on. So, moral discourse is both disciplined and has the requisite syntactic features.

It follows that if minimalism about truth-aptness is correct then moral claims *are* the sorts of things that can be true or false. By arriving at this conclusion we have done what the quasi-realist wanted: we have not needed to discuss anything about belief, moral property or description. The quasi-realist can use minimalism about truth-aptness to secure from a non-cognitivist starting point one of the central realist-seeming features of our moral practice – truth-aptness. It is no surprise then that quasi-realists would find minimalism about truth-aptness attractive.

However, if we consider what we have discussed thus far in this section a worry emerges. Think about the question that started this section: "What identifies a non-cognitivist?" We answered this with the claim that a non-cognitivist holds that moral judgements are *not* truth-apt.

However, there seems good reason for the quasi-realist to accept minimalism about truth-aptness and in doing so accept that moral judgements *are* truth-apt. But if they do this, it seems quasi-realists will struggle to identify themselves as non-cognitivists. There is a danger that quasi-realism has, in Blackburn's phrase, "bitten its own tail". Wright sums up this challenge:

> Either [quasi-realism] fails – in which case [the *quasi*-realist] does not, after all, explain how the [non-cognitivism] that inspires it can satisfactorily account for the linguistic practices in question [e.g. talk of truth-aptness] – or it succeeds, in which case it makes good all the things the [non-cognitivist] started out wanting to deny: that the discourse in question is genuinely assetoric, aimed at truth and so on.   (1987: 35)

The reader should ask how the quasi-realist might respond to this sort of challenge. One route is to characterize non-cognitivism as the view that moral judgements are truth-apt but express non-descriptive beliefs. This contrasts with cognitivism, which claims that moral judgments are truth-apt and express descriptive beliefs. This distinction between descriptive and non-descriptive beliefs would mean that cognitivism and non-cognitivism are in opposite camps.

Of course, this raises the question: what on earth are "non-descriptive" beliefs? We shall pursue this a little when we discuss Terry Horgan and Mark Timmons's non-descriptive cognitivism in Chapter 10. What is clear, though, is that if Blackburn can adequately show that moral judgments express non-descriptive beliefs, then he can better show how to respect the realist features of moral practice while remaining true to non-cognitivism.

Conclusion

Non-cognitivism seemed highly attractive in the light of Moore's OQA since it could respect the insight of his argument regarding the practical nature of moral judgements without accepting his realist conclusions about non-natural properties. However, the Frege–Geach problem seems to completely undermine non-cognitivism so that we are left with anti-realism and cognitivism, but this is error theory (Chapter 3). Blackburn takes on the task of explaining how to defend non-cognitivism in light of these worries, and argues that although non-cognitivism is right, we can also explain why we act and talk like cognitivists.

We suggested a dilemma for quasi-realism. Either it is correct and we cannot identify non-cognitivism as non-cognitivism, or we can identify non-cognitivism but quasi-realism cannot capture all the features of our moral practice. To give an example, minimalism about truth-aptness allows the quasi-realist to say that moral judgements *are* truth-apt but in doing so rules out the key way of demarcating non-cognitivism from cognitivism.

We ended with the suggestion that we could avoid this dilemma if the quasi-realist could claim that moral judgements express non-descriptive beliefs. Arguably, taking this route would mean that the quasi-realist could show how the non-cognitivist could respect moral practice but at the same time allow a way of demarcating non-cognitivism from cognitivism.

THINGS TO REMEMBER

- The non-cognitivists do not believe that we *speak* a different moral language.
- The Frege–Geach problem occurs anywhere there are asserted and unasserted contexts; in particular, it can occur outside cases of *modus ponens*.
- Quasi-realism is a commitment to a certain explanatory programme rather than a position.
- Minimalism about truth-aptness is not the same as minimalism about truth.

Further reading

For a good summary of Frege–Geach problem and Blackburn's response see Miller (2003: chs 3, 4). For a summary of the Frege–Geach problem, including its historical context, see Schroeder (2008) and for a more detailed account see Schroeder (2010). For a good summary of anti-realism see Blackburn (2007) and for a collection of his papers dealing with quasi-realism see Blackburn (1993). For a good survey of the recent developments in expressivism see Sinclair (2009). A good account of minimalism about truth-aptness, truth and realism can be found in Miller (2007: ch. 9).

7

Moral relativism

[Relativism is] possibly the most absurd view to have been advanced even in
moral philosophy.   (Williams 1972: 34)

The aim of most philosophical discussions of relativism is to establish its mani-
fest falsity.   (Wong 2006: xi)

I have always been a moral relativist. As far back as I can remember thinking
about it, it has always seemed to me obvious that the dictates of morality arise
from some sort of convention or understandings, and that there are no basic
moral demands that apply to everyone. For many years this seemed so obvious
to me that I assumed it was everyone's instinctive view, at least everyone who
gave the matter any thought.   (Harman 2000: 77)

CHAPTER AIMS

- To outline speaker and agent relativism and distinguish between
  them.
- To outline the motivations for relativism.
- To pose a problem for both speaker and agent relativism.
- To show how issues relating to relativism are also related to discussions
  of meaning, truth and external reasons.

Introduction

Relativism could do with a good spin-doctor. In philosophical discussions if you can show your opponent holds a relativist position then you
have as good as won. Calling someone a "relativist" is rarely a compli-
ment and even professional philosophers tend to write as if being able
to demonstrate that a position leads to relativism is enough to question
the truth of that position. This is unfair. "Relativism" covers a multitude of sophisticated and widely defended positions and although we
cannot consider them all, we shall discuss two: *speaker relativism* and
agent relativism. I have chosen these two because they highlight a broad

spectrum of metaethical issues and get to the heart of some of the most pressing questions that face most forms of relativism.

Agent relativism

The agent relativist argues that someone's action is right or wrong depending on his or her moral framework. So, for example, John protesting against animal testing is right if and only if protesting against animal testing is prescribed by *John's* moral framework. This is *relativism* because an action may be right in relation to one person's framework but wrong in relation to another's. In our example, protesting against animal testing might be right for John because of his moral framework, but wrong for Tim given his, and right for Matt given his.

A moral framework is a set of rules telling us how to react in different situations generated by the values, standards and principles we hold. For instance, we might believe that life is sacred and hence have a rule outlawing abortion, or we might believe that charity is more important than luxury and choose to help Oxfam.

We should be clear that agent relativism is not the position that what is right and wrong is whatever anyone chooses or that we have moral licence to do anything simply because we want it enough. This is for the simple reason that what we choose might be out of line with what is prescribed by our own framework. And if what we choose is not prescribed by our framework then – according to agent relativism – what we do will be morally wrong.

Moral frameworks are generated by the values, standards and principles we hold and consequently they will be dependent on the contexts in which people find themselves. For instance, if we were brought up by secular, liberal parents we might have a rule allowing abortion whereas if we were brought up by Catholic parents we would not have such a rule. There are two important things here: first, the relativist claims that there is no shared universal framework; second, it makes no sense to say one moral framework is "more *correct*" than another.

We can start to see why agent relativism might be correct if we consider a number of examples. These examples are meant to get us to begin to think about what needs to be in place for someone's actions to be right or wrong.

(a) In 2010 an oil rig sank in the Gulf of Mexico. The resultant oil spill was recorded as the biggest environmental catastrophe in US history, killing hundreds of thousands of plants and animals. The oil led to a depletion of the world's natural habitat. This was a terrible event. Do we think that what the *oil* did was *morally* wrong?

(b) On Christmas day in 2007 Tatiana the tiger escaped from San Francisco Zoo, because of a low enclosure wall, and killed a visitor and injured another. What happened was horrific. Was what the *tiger* did *morally* wrong?

(c) In October 2009, UK *X Factor* winner Leona Lewis was at a book signing in London when someone broke through security and punched her in the head. After he was arrested it became apparent that the attacker was suffering from a serious mental illness. Such violence is awful, but did the *attacker* do something *morally* wrong?

How might we answer these questions? Given that oil is not even an *agent* it is hard to make sense of the claim that what the oil did was wrong. If we thought that what the oil did was wrong, we would have to start blaming all manner of inanimate objects for their "actions"; for instance, the bed on which I stubbed my toe, the hammer that hit my finger, the banister that gave me a splinter and so on. This would be silly. The oil did not do anything morally wrong.

What about the tiger? Well I submit that most people would say that even though it was a horrific event, what the tiger did was not morally wrong. This is different from the oil case because tigers are conscious and aware of their surroundings. We can talk about tigers *wanting* to maul someone, or even perhaps – at a stretch – *intending* to maul someone. However, simply being conscious, wanting and intending is not enough to guarantee that we can apportion blame. In the case of the tiger, we do not blame it for what it did. We do not think that a tiger, or any other animal, is a moral agent and that its actions can be right or wrong. Therefore, having considered these two examples, we can say that if something is inanimate or falls short of having the mental capabilities of a human then they *cannot* act morally.

Things get tougher in our third example regarding the attack on Leona Lewis. Much can and has been said about these sorts of issues (e.g. Arenella 1990; Haji 1998; Rosen 2003; Guerrero 2007). However, intuitively we are likely to think that what the attacker did was not morally wrong as he was suffering from a severe mental illness. Arguing that this was a horrible thing to happen is not the same as claiming that the attacker's action was morally wrong. It seems that we think this because, given the attacker's illness and subsequent limited mental ability, moral considerations are somehow *beyond* him.

Thinking through these examples, it seems there might be a continuum. At one end are inanimate objects, which clearly cannot do anything wrong; then there are animals – which, although conscious, are not capable of wrong either; then there are people who have diminished mental capacities – we would have to look at each case of these in turn. Then presumably at the far end of the continuum are normally functioning adults whose actions can, of course, be right or wrong. For instance, if a normally functioning adult punched someone in the head then we would have no hesitation in judging that what they did was morally wrong.

If this is true then perhaps the agent relativist is onto something. What this continuum suggests is that the varied mental capacities of those carrying out an action will impact on whether their action is right or wrong. Importantly this means that we cannot say that a certain *type of action* is right or wrong without qualification.

Yet once we have recognized that the rightness or wrongness of actions will depend on certain criteria regarding the agent, we are forced to consider these criteria in more detail. The agent relativist's point is that an agent's moral framework should be part of these criteria and should be integral to our judgement. We shall develop this by considering some thoughts from Gilbert Harman (2000).

Imagine an agent who is considering whether or not to perform an action. She gets as much information as she possibly can, thinks long and hard about it and in the end decides to do it. Now, she has carefully considered all aspects and made her decision, which nobody would be able to change: in this case we might want to say that there is no reason for the agent not to perform the action.

Furthermore, since we tie the question of whether someone's action is right and wrong into the notion of reason, then in this case if the agent performs the action then we are unable to say that she *ought* not to have performed it, since we have established that there is no reason for her not to do so. This means we cannot say that she has done something wrong in performing the action. Based on an example from Harman, and granting me some artistic licence, we shall make this less abstract.

Imagine you are part of a round table discussion with Hitler and his top-ranking officials. The meeting is about whether to enact the "final solution", in which there would be a systematic and maintained effort to murder all Jewish people. After listening for a while, you start to interject by giving what you see as patently obvious reasons why they should not carry out this horrific action. However, whatever reasons you bring to the table, whatever arguments you give, however many facts you cite, they just do not understand. They are listening, but they shake their heads when you speak and look at you blankly. You say, "But all people are equal! The Jewish people have the same right to life as you or me."

They respond, "But Jewish people aren't in the same category as everyone else."

"But you will bring about great suffering!", you say.

They answer, "Some suffering is surely worth it for the greater good", and so on.

Hitler and his cronies can see no possible reason not to enact the "final solution". There are no deliberations they could go through such that they would be motivated not to give the order. They continue with their appalling plan.

The question to ask yourself is whether you think that *Hitler* has a reason *not* to carry out the order. Agent relativists such as Harman would say he has not, since no amount of deliberation would change his mind. If there is no way of persuading Hitler, then it makes no sense to claim that Hitler has a reason not to give the order. So if Hitler has no reason not to give the order then it cannot make sense to say that he *ought* not to give the order. How odd it would be to claim that "Hitler ought not to give the order but there is no reason for him not to give the order." Yet if we cannot say he ought not to give the order then it seems we cannot claim that it was *wrong* of him to give the order. If all this is right, Hitler did not do anything morally wrong in giving the order to murder the Jewish people.

This is quite some conclusion! Lest people start sending hate mail to agent relativists, we must be clear that in such an example, the agent relativist is not condoning Hitler's actions. Harman explicitly says that what Hitler did was a "great evil". Moreover, we stipulated many things to make the example work. The point, though, is that if we charitably granted these points, given Hitler's moral framework, we cannot say that what Hitler (the agent) did was morally wrong.

Comparing Hitler's actions to a case where a tiger attacked some children, Harman puts it like this:

> Suppose Mabel takes Hitler's actions to be a great evil and also believes that *Hitler's values were sufficiently perverse that they provided Hitler with no reason to refrain from acting as he acted.* Mabel may then view Hitler as in some ways similar to the tiger. Although she judges Hitler to be a great evil she finds she is no more able to judge that it was wrong *of* Hitler to have acted as he acted than to judge that it was wrong *of* the tiger to have attacked the children.   (2000: 60, emphasis added)

Therefore it seems that someone's moral framework might determine whether *that* person's actions are right or wrong. Given that there are many moral frameworks and no standard by which to say one is better than another, we cannot say that an action is right or wrong without further qualification. That is to say, we should accept agent relativism.

A problem for agent relativism

There are many hugely complicated issues surrounding agent relativism and we shall briefly look at one. This issue introduces a wider and more general metaethical issue, that of internal and external reasons, and in order to understand why we must return to the argument regarding Hitler.

In our Harman-inspired example, we claimed that given Hitler's perverse moral framework, if there was nothing that we could do to convince Hitler so that he would be motivated to stop giving the order, then we *cannot* say that Hitler has a reason to stop giving the order. This inability to deliberate from his current motivations so as to be motivated not to give the order led us to conclude that we cannot claim he has a reason not to give the order. This claim about the necessary link between an agent's reasons and an agent's motivational set is the claim that *all* reasons are internal reasons.

What is worth underlining is that the "deliberation" involved must be from the agent's current motivations. So for the agent relativist argument to work it must be the case that from Hitler's current motivations there is no deliberation he could undertake that would mean he was motivated not to give the order.

To understand the agent relativist's argument better and because philosophers distinguish between motivating and normative reasons, we need to make sure we know which ones are meant to be internal. Does the agent relativist argument rely on the claim that motivating reasons are internal reasons or that all normative reasons are internal? The answer is the latter. In order for the argument in support of agent relativism to work, all normative reasons need to be internal. Let us then clarify the distinction between motivating and normative reasons.

Motivating reasons are those reasons we possess that explain the actions we perform. For example, if I have a motivating reason to dive into the bubbling hot spring in the National Park then this explains my swimming. If I have a motivating reason to practice my riposte in fencing then this explains the practice routine I adopt.

However, these differ from normative reasons and we shall continue with the swimming example to understand why. Suppose I have not realized that the spring in the park is 110°C and would kill me if I dived in. In such a case, it seems quite natural to say that there is a reason for me *not* to jump in. Philosophers call such a reason a normative reason. Despite the fact that I have a motivating reason to jump – I want to swim – there is a normative reason for me not to jump. Of course these reasons *can* converge. If I learnt of the temperature of the water then the normative reason would also be my motivating reason. But they are conceptually distinct and we are only concerned with normative reasons.

This means that if we can show that there could be a normative reason that is not an internal reason, we could challenge agent relativism. To spell this out: if there is a reason for an agent to act in a certain way, even though he could not, after deliberation from his current motivations, be motivated by it, then this would challenge agent

---

Bernard Williams (1929–2003)

- Knightbridge Professor of Philosophy at the University of Cambridge.
- Key text: *Ethics and The Limits of Philosophy* (1985).
- The key claim: normative reasons are internal reasons. If someone has a reason to act in a certain way, then that person has some motive that will be served by doing that action. Williams rejects the possibility of external reasons.

relativism. The view that this is possible is the view that some normative reasons are external reasons.

And in fact it does seem, contrary to what agent relativists think, that external reasons do exist. Consider an example inspired by Shafer-Landau (2003) who in turn was inspired by Millgram (1996). In Roger Hargreaves's "Little Miss" books there is a character called "Little Miss Shy". She

> was so shy she just couldn't bring herself to leave her little cottage. She never went shopping! The thought of walking into a shop and asking for something was absolutely terrifying. So, she grew her own food in the garden of Thimble Cottage, and lived a very quiet life. Very, very, very, very quiet indeed.
>
> (1981: 3)

To cut the story short, after sleepless nights and lots of worry she ends up at Mr Funny's party. At this party she starts to feel unwell and restless. But "everyone talked to her, and everyone was very nice, and gradually, the longer the party lasted, bit by bit, little by little, eventually, guess what happened? She stopped blushing. And actually started to enjoy herself" (*ibid*.: 14). Although she faints, overall she has a good time and starts to make friends with Mr Quiet – her first ever friend.

If we asked Little Miss Shy a few weeks later if she thought she had *had* a reason to go the party, she would probably say yes. She can now see that as a result of going to the party she has more of a life, she has made some friends, has started new projects and had lots of new experiences. She might add that all this would not have happened if she had not been brave enough to go to the party.

To make this into a challenge to agent relativism we need to ask whether *before* she went to the party Little Miss Shy could have deliberated such that she would be motivated to go. Arguably this was not possible. When she received the invite she felt sick and lost sleep and given the *type* of person she was, it seems that there was no way she could deliberate such that she would be motivated to go to the party.

Here, then, is the challenge to the agent relativist's argument. If we think that Little Miss Shy *did* have a reason to go to the party but that there was no way of her coming to be motivated to go to the party, then we think that she has a normative reason to go to the party; a normative reason which is *not* an internal reason. In other words, external reasons do exist. Although this is a children's story we do not need much imagination to see how this might map onto everyday cases. As Shafer-Landau writes:

> It is true of many different kinds of people that if they were somehow to "look beyond" the picture of things they have grown used to, they would find themselves with an outlook, a plan of life, and a set of circumstances that they would find more valuable than *they could ever have imagined*. In such cases, realizing the relevant benefits often requires a *change of character* … the goodness available only to those who make such changes may be so valuable as to make it true that one has, *despite one's present motivations, a reason* to make the necessary changes.   (2003: 186, emphasis added)

So to put these thoughts back into the Hitler example, if external reasons do exist then we can claim that there *is* a reason for Hitler not to give the order, despite the fact that there may be no way of him being able to deliberate from his current motivations such that he would be motivated not to give the order. Therefore, despite Hitler's moral framework prescribing the giving of the order, there may still be a way of saying he ought not to give the order, and that if he did he would have done something morally wrong. This of course, would be in direct conflict with agent relativism.

There are many issues about internal and external reasons, and normative and motivating reasons (see Further Reading below for a way into these discussions). There are also many other things we could ask about agent relativism in general and the Hitler example in particular. However, we shall now turn to consider speaker relativism.

Speaker relativism

Q: Why did the chicken cross the road?
Einstein's answer: Did the chicken really cross the road or did the road move beneath the chicken?

Some claims are relative. For example, if asked whether London is dangerous, we are likely to respond, "Well, it depends: relative to St

Andrews yes, relative to Kabul no." Or, when asked if Ferrari's new production car is *fast*, we are likely to respond: "Relative to my bike yes, relative to a jet fighter no."

The interesting question is whether we should treat moral claims as relative in a similar way. For example, when we judge that "killing is wrong", do we think this is true for all people across all times and cultures? Or is it best understood as being relative to a speaker's moral framework? The *speaker relativist* argues for the latter and thinks that no moral claim is true absolutely.

But why is this different from the *agent* relativism we have just discussed? Consider an example. If I say, "The action of the rebel soldiers in Darfur is morally wrong", then the speaker relativist would be interested in my moral framework as the speaker.

On the other hand, the agent relativist would focus on the soldiers' actions as moral agents. The agent relativist believes that the soldiers' actions would be right or wrong depending on whether they are prescribed by the soldiers' moral framework.

It seems possible then that the speaker relativist could correctly judge that the soldiers' actions are morally wrong because of the speaker's moral framework, while the agent relativist judges that the soldiers' actions are morally right because of the soldiers' moral framework. Let us consider some further qualifications of speaker relativism.

According to speaker relativism, when I make a moral judgement what I am saying is elliptical and can only be judged as true or false in relation to my moral framework. However, we must be careful here to distinguish relational and relative. People who reject relativism can still *compare* moral actions and hence make moral claims that are relational. For example, they might hold that in relation to stealing, murder is more despicable, or that in relation to hanging, the lethal injection is a preferable method of execution.

This, though, *is not* what we mean by relativism. We can illustrate this if we think about how the non-relativist and the relativist would differ about the truth of the claims we just considered. Consider the claims "in relation to stealing, murder is more despicable" and "in relation to hanging, the lethal injection is a preferable method of execution". For the non-relativist these claims will be true or false, irrespective of who is speaking: that is, the truth or falsity of these claims cuts across people's varying moral frameworks. However, for the relativist the truth of these relational claims will be dependent on people's moral frameworks. So, for instance, if I claim that "in relation to stealing, murder is more despicable" this might be true; whereas if you claim it, it might be false.

Is speaker relativism correct? If we consider how people actually talk, speaker relativism seems *prima facie* false: that is, when people make moral claims they do not mean what they say to be taken as relative. For example, when someone condemns the treatment of prisoners in Guantánamo Bay, he does not qualify his judgement with "It's true for me, but it may not be true for you"; and when Osama bin Laden called "the West" a "great evil", he did not mean this to be prefixed with "For me …". When making moral claims we do not mean them to be relative, and consequently speaker relativism seems to be incorrect.

Of course, the speaker relativist will want to claim that *despite* what we mean when we speak, the theory is still correct. This would seem to commit speaker relativism to the unattractive claim that because we mean one thing, and the truth is something different, every time we make moral claims what we say is systematically and uniformly false. Because of how we speak, the speaker relativist is then seemingly forced to accept either that his theory is false or that it is an error theory.

Speaker relativists think that they can avoid the horns of this dilemma by thinking harder about the conditions under which a moral claim is true. Specifically, they distinguish between what people *mean* by their moral claims and a moral claim's truth-conditions. This gives them space to hold that even though we do not intend a moral claim to be relative, the truth of the moral claim might be relative. For example, the speaker relativist would say that even though when I say "Torturing prisoners is morally wrong" I do not mean "For *me*, torturing prisoners is morally wrong", the truth of whether it is wrong to torture prisoners will depend on my moral framework.

This is a fine line for the speaker relativist to walk, for we might think that there is some intimate connection between what a claim means and the conditions under which the claim can be said to be true.

The important point here is that we *cannot* defeat speaker relativism simply by pointing out that people do not speak and think as relativists, because the truth of our moral claims may be relative despite our language not wearing its relativism on its sleeve.

Moral disagreement: a reason to adopt speaker relativism and a reason to reject it

It seems that there can be moral disagreements where *no one* is at fault. It is an intuitive idea that however much information people have, however rational people are, they might still disagree. For example, we can imagine two rational and well-educated people – one a Catholic and one a non-Catholic – disagreeing about abortion. Moreover, we can imagine the disagreement continuing despite the emergence of new information or an increase in deliberation and discussion.

If we were moral realists and thought that there were moral *properties* this would be a big problem, and therefore moral disagreement is often used as an argument against realism. For if there were moral properties which could be accessed – say, for example, the wrongness of abortion – we would think that it is at least possible that the Catholic and non-Catholic could come to agree about the wrongness of abortion. To put it another way, if there are moral properties then it seems that any disagreement will be due to a fault in people's reasoning or cognitive powers. So moral realism seemingly has no place for faultless moral disagreement and consequently would have to explain, or explain away, the belief that there can be faultless moral disagreements.

In contrast, the relativist can respect the intuition that such disagreements are possible. Going back to our example, the relativist would argue that the Catholic and non-Catholic have *different* moral frameworks that determine the truth of their moral claims. This means that because of the values that the Catholic has and the values that the non-Catholic has, their judgements will never converge. They are not making a mistake about some fact, or reasoning incorrectly. Because they have different frames of reference, they will not agree. If relativism is correct then faultless moral disagreements are only to be expected.

The relativist is not committed to it being impossible to have moral agreement, for two people could disagree but share the *same moral framework*. In this case reflection, discussion and considering the facts would resolve the disagreement. For example, if two Catholics disagree about abortion, through discussion and reflection one might realize that he had not fully understood the implication of his own moral framework and come into line with the other. It seems then that speaker relativism fits well with our everyday experiences of moral disagreement.

We might think that if speaker relativism is right then the meaning of moral claims will be relative to the moral framework people have: that is, that when I make a moral claim I am *referring to* my framework, and when you make a moral claim you are *referring to* yours. To return to our example, when the Catholic says "abortion is wrong" he means that "abortion is wrong *for me*", and when the non-Catholic says "abortion is not wrong" he means "abortion is not wrong *for me*".

Yet if is right then we have *lost* disagreement, for disagreement depends on shared meaning. If I say "my mouse squeaks", and you say "no it doesn't", and we then find out that I am talking about my pet mouse and you are talking about my computer mouse, we would conclude that there is no disagreement. In our moral example, if the Catholic means "abortion is wrong for me" and the non-Catholic means "abortion is not wrong for me" then they are *not* disagreeing but talking at cross-purposes (we raised similar issues when we discussed emotivism, subjectivism and relativism in Chapter 2). This is a major problem for the speaker relativist. Ragnar Francén puts the problem like this: "The problem for moral speaker relativism is that it makes moral assertions made by speakers with different moralities be about *different things* (express different propositions), and that they therefore *do not disagree* in the intuitive sense when they are involved in moral disputes" (2009: 26, emphasis added).

However, the speaker relativists are confident that they have a response to this challenge. They would refer to the claim we made in the last section, where we noted that speaker relativists split *meaning* from *truth-conditions*. If this is a possibility then this would allow people from different moral frameworks to disagree, while relativism remained true. There would be genuine disagreement because their moral claims could have a common meaning and consequently they would not be talking at cross-purposes. Yet they would still be relativists because the truth of those claims would be relative to the speaker's moral framework.

If this move is possible then the speaker relativist could say that there is a *common* meaning between the Catholic and non-Catholic, despite their radically different moral frameworks. If there is a shared meaning, they can genuinely disagree and need not be talking at cross-purposes. The relativism comes in because for the Catholic "abortion is wrong" is true relative to *his* moral framework whereas for the non-Catholic "abortion is not wrong" is true relative to *his* moral framework. It seems therefore that the speaker relativist can hold on to relativism while explaining disagreement. John MacFarlane sums this up (although he talks in terms of "propositions" we can for the sake of argument read this as "meaning"):

> One might … despair of ever getting [*speaker relativism*] and *disagreement* into the same picture. Perhaps we just have to choose? This is where the relativist comes in with her seductive song. "You can have it both ways," she says, "if you just accept that [moral] propositions … have *truth values* relative to a person or perspective. When I say that [abortion is wrong] and you deny this, you are denying the *very same proposition* that I am asserting. *We genuinely disagree. Yet this proposition may be true for you and false for me.*"
>
> (2007: 23–4, emphasis added)

So if the relativist can show that meaning can remain constant but that the truth-conditions vary, then they can hold on to moral disagreement and relativism. Can they show that? This is a tough and controversial question to try to answer but I shall just make a few comments as to why they might struggle.

This response by the speaker relativist is controversial because it conflicts with a fairly intuitive idea that the *meaning* of a sentence determines the conditions under which it is true. For instance, you might think that what determines whether the claim "Je suis heureux" is true or false will depend on its *meaning*. If it means "I am happy" it is true, if it means "I am a tomato" then it is false. David Lewis puts this intuitive thought more formally:

> A meaning for a sentence is something that determines the conditions under which the sentence is true or false. It determines the truth-value of the sentence in various possible states of affairs, at various times, at various places, for various speakers, and so on.
> (1972: 173)

Although this view can be, and has been, questioned, if it can be defended the speaker relativist has a problem. If the speaker relativist claims that where people have different moral frameworks there can be a common meaning, and if meaning determines the truth-conditions, then it seems that the speaker relativist is committed to there being common truth-conditions across cases of different moral frameworks. But then, of course, it is a mystery why their position should now be called *relativism*. If truth and meaning are not relative to individual moral frameworks, what is left for them to be relativist about?

So the speaker relativist has to respond to this challenge either by denying the link between meaning and truth-conditions or by giving up one of the main attractions of speaker relativism: namely the ability to explain how we can have faultless moral disagreement.

Conclusion

Relativism is more complex and sophisticated than is often thought. There are many different versions of relativism and we have focused on just two: agent relativism and speaker relativism.

Agent relativism claims that if an agent's moral framework prescribes a certain action then that action would be right if the agent performed it. Although it seemed plausible that the moral standards we judge agents by are related to the agent's mental capabilities, it also seemed that the agent relativist's position led to some counter-intuitive conclusions. To see one potential problem at the heart of agent relativism, we introduced the debate between internal and external reason theorists, a central issue in metaethics.

Speaker relativism asked us to focus on the speaker's moral framework rather than the moral framework of the agent performing the action. Speaker relativism gained its plausibility from the fact that it seems possible that there is faultless moral disagreement. One concern is that in order for the speaker relativist to keep moral disagreement she would need common meaning across people's moral frameworks. This means that if the intuitive idea that meaning determines truth-conditions is correct, speaker relativism would also be committed to there being common truth-conditions across frameworks. It then would be up to the relativists to articulate what their relativism amounts to.

Consequently it seems that the speaker relativist has either to show that there is common meaning across frameworks or to abandon the possibility of genuine moral disagreement.

THINGS TO REMEMBER

- People who reject relativism can still compare moral actions and hence make moral claims that are *relational*.
- Relativism not only states that moral claims are judged relative to a moral framework but also that there is no *one* true moral framework.
- The relativist does not think that disagreement itself leads to relativism. Moral disagreement is a challenge that non-relativists have to explain.
- We cannot defeat speaker relativism simply by pointing out that people do not speak and think as relativists, because the truth of our moral claims may be relative despite our language not wearing its relativism on its sleeve.

Further reading

The *locus classicus* regarding internal and external reasons is Williams (1981). For a good discussion of internal and external reasons see Shafer-Landau (2003: pt IV). For a tougher paper attacking internal reasons see Lillehammer (2000). For a classic debate about relativism see Harman & Thomson (1996). For an overview of relativism see Blackburn (2000); for a short introduction to moral relativism see Levy (2002). Boghossian (2006b) is a paper on what relativism is and Hales (2011) is a collection of papers on relativism. For a tough extended discussion of disagreement see Tersman (2006). For a discussion of truth conditions and meaning see Miller (2007).

8

Moral psychology

When asked if he wore the skin face masks over a prolonged time: "Not too long, I had other things to do." Ed Gein (murderer and grave robber)

CHAPTER AIMS

- Explain internalism and externalism about motivation.
- Explain the Humean account of motivation.
- Explain the implications from issues in moral psychology.
- Outline some potential worries for discussions about moral psychology.

Introduction: not "getting it"

The [psychopath] is unfamiliar with the primary facts or data of what might be called personal values and is *altogether inca-pable of understanding* such matters. It is impossible for him to take even the slightest interest in the tragedy or joy or the striving of humanity as presented in serious literature or art. He is also indifferent to all these matters in life itself. Beauty and ugliness, except in a very superficial sense, goodness, evil, love, horror, and humor have *no actual meaning, no power to move him*. He is, furthermore, lacking in the ability to see that others are moved. It is as though he were *color-blind*, despite his sharp intelligence, to this aspect of human existence. It cannot be explained to him because there is nothing in his orbit of awareness that can bridge the gap with comparison. *He can repeat the words and say glibly that he understands, and there is no way for him to realize that he does not understand.*

(Cleckley 1941: 90, emphasis added)

What makes us different from the psychopath? What do we "get" that they do not? What does the psychopath lack when considered as a *moral* agent? In this chapter we shall explore these questions and what the best explanation could be for why moral judgements can motivate us.

One thing that is so shocking and perplexing about psychopaths is that they are detached and indifferent to moral considerations. They remain unmoved and unconcerned about whether something is right, wrong, good, bad, praiseworthy, evil and so on. Pleading with them on moral grounds is futile. Other concerns guide them: how to be noticed, how to fulfil sexual desires, how to make money and so on. In contrast, judging that it is wrong to kill is sufficient reason for most people to move them not to do it. It is not necessary that the law or society also forbids it. Judging that killing is *morally* wrong is enough to influence behaviour.

Yet what is this link to motivation? Consider what we might say of the killer Ed Gein. Gein claimed that he understood that wearing dead skin masks from corpses and making soup bowls from scalps was wrong, but could not see what that had to do with how he behaved. Is he, to borrow the phrase from the quotation above, just repeating the words and saying he understands when in fact he does not? Or, in contrast, do we think he *understands* but just does not care about being moral?

It is not just abnormal psychology that is relevant. Imagine discussing the fur trade with a sane friend and apparently convincing them that wearing fur was morally wrong. The next day we see them dressed in a mink coat, squirrel hat and bearskin boots. This baffles us and we remind them of the previous day's conversation. They respond: "I know that it is wrong to wear fur, but why should I care about that?"

We would be puzzled, just as with the psychopath, and might try to rationalize why our friend had acted in such a way. Whatever we decide is the reason for her behaviour, what does become apparent is that we require an explanation of the link between moral judgement and motivation.

The possible explanation: internalism versus externalism about motivation

There are two key alternative explanations of how judgements are linked to motivation. The first is the *internalist explanation*, which holds that as a matter of conceptual necessity moral judgements motivate; the internalist believes it is conceptually impossible for someone to make a genuine moral judgement yet fail to be motivated. Therefore the internalist will claim that because the psychopath and the fur wearer were not motivated, then she knows *a priori* that neither made a genuine moral judgement.

Many metaethicists, for example Michael Smith (1994), adopt a weaker form of internalism. It is weaker because although there is still a necessary connection between judgement and motivation, it allows for cases where agents make genuine moral judgements but still are *not* motivated. For the weak internalist this is possible in those cases where the agent is suffering from depression, weakness of will or the like. However, we shall continue our discussion with the stronger form outlined in the previous paragraph.

Second is the *externalist explanation*, which holds that if moral judgements motivate then this is in virtue of the agent's desires. This means that the motivation is external to the moral judgment and consequently, given that an agent may or may not have the desire, moral judgements may or may not motivate. For the externalist, then, the link between moral judgement and motivation is contingent and not necessary. So the externalist would say, for example, that if I judge it is right to give money to charity then only *if* I have a desire to give money to charity will I be motivated to do so. Yet of course it is possible that I may not have the desire and consequently may not be motivated by my judgement.

Therefore the key difference between the internalist and the externalist is that the internalist thinks that the link between moral judgement and motivation is necessary while the externalist thinks the link is contingent. (Some have tried to find a middle ground between these positions; see e.g. Simpson [1999].)

How, then, are we to decide between the internalist and externalist? This is an extremely difficult question to answer. This is because the internalist claims that we can describe *any* possible case where judgement fails to motivate as a case where the moral judgement is *not* genuine. This means that the supposed counter-examples are not in fact counter-examples, since they are not cases where *genuine* judgement fails to motivate. In such cases the internalist will say that when the agent makes a moral judgement they are in fact imitating or mimicking moral practice; Hare (1952) calls this making a moral judgement in an *inverted comma* sense. For example, the internalist will claim that when our friend says that although it is wrong to wear fur she has no motivation not to wear it, she has not made a genuine judgement. Rather, when she says "Wearing fur is wrong", she actually means "Wearing fur is what *people around me* would judge as wrong" or "Wearing fur is what *society* would judge wrong". So in this case a genuine moral judgement has not failed to motivate, and hence we do not need to reject internalism. The internalist thinks that they can repeat this process for *any* possible case where motivation fails to follow from apparently genuine moral judgement.

On the other hand, the externalist has no problem with claiming that moral judgements can be genuine but may fail to motivate. In fact, they would claim that we would sometimes expect people to make genuine moral judgements without being motivated because our desires can often change. In our example, they would say that our fur wearer *does* make a genuine moral judgement but lacks an appropriate desire and hence fails to be motivated. Obviously we cannot advance the debate between internalists and externalists merely by introducing more and more examples but before looking for a way to continue we do need to say a bit more about these positions.

Four clarifications: psychology, action, reasons and amoralism

First, the debate between internalism and externalism is about the link between moral judgement and motivation and not about whether *true* judgements motivate. So, for example, it is not relevant to the debate to claim that some people judge that it is great to skin babies, or lynch people or deprive people of a fair trial and so on and are still motivated to do such horrible things, because the question still remains as to what best explains the link between judgement and motivation. Demonstrating that *false* moral claims can motivate does not advance the debate.

Second, for us, the key question is whether people can fail to be motivated to do what they judge to be right, *not* whether they fail to *do* what is right, for motivation and action are distinct. For example, we might be motivated to buy Fairtrade chocolate because we believe it is right but fail to actually buy any. Internalism and externalism concern *motivation*, not action.

Third, there is a debate in metaethics that concerns reasons and centres on what is the best explanation of the link between moral judgements and reasons for action. The *internalist* about reasons claims that the link is necessary; the *externalist* about reasons claims that it is contingent. (This is a different debate from the one we discussed in the last chapter regarding internal and external reasons.) However, what we are interested in is motivation and *not* practical reason.

Finally, in this debate "amoralist" has a precise meaning. In particular it does not just mean someone who is nasty or thinks morality is irrelevant. Rather, the "amoralist" is defined as someone who makes *genuine* moral judgements and is psychologically "normal" but who fails to be motivated by a particular judgement. In fact, given this definition metaethicists sometimes frame the debate between the internalist and externalist in terms of the possible existence of the amoralist. Because the internalist thinks that there is a conceptually *necessary* link between judgement and motivation, she thinks that the amoralist is conceptually *impossible*, while the externalist thinks that they are possible.

Michael Smith's argumentative strategy

Michael Smith (1994: Chapter 3) has probably done more than anyone else to bring the issue of internalism and externalism into focus in contemporary metaethics.

We said above that there was a problem in trying to advance the debate between internalism and externalism. Smith suggests a way of proceeding. He thinks we should identify something that *both* the internalist and the externalist would agree on and then show how only *one* position can explain it.

Smith thinks both internalists and externalists would agree on what he calls "the striking fact". This is the contingent empirical claim that "a *change in motivation* follows reliably in the wake of a *change in moral judgement*" (1994: 71, emphasis added). This seems generally to be true. For example, if I judged it right to vote for the Republicans then I would be motivated to do so. If I changed my mind and thought it was right to vote for the Democrats then I would be motivated to vote for them instead. One might think that the externalist should not accept the striking fact because it somehow favours internalism. However, the "striking fact" is silent about the *nature* of the link between judgement and motivation. All it says is that typically it seems that if people change their judgement then their motivation also changes. So if both the internalist and externalist would accept the striking fact then we should adopt the one that is best able to account for it. As we shall see, Smith argues that this is internalism.

Internalism versus externalism: do externalists get our moral psychology wrong?

Smith argues that the internalist has no problem in explaining the striking fact. For the internalist, a change in motivation reliably follows a change in judgement because there is a *necessary link* between judgement and motivation, so it would follow that a change in judgement brings with it a change in motivation. For example, if I judge it right to see Beth then necessarily I shall be motivated to see her. If I change my mind and judge it right to see Freya then necessarily I shall be motivated to see her. So the internalist has no problem accounting for the striking fact. However, Smith thinks that the externalist has a less plausible explanation.

What explains the link for the externalist between judgement and motivation is the *desires* of the *agent*. So, for example, if I judge it right to see Beth and if I *desire* to do the right thing then I shall be motivated to see her. How then will the externalist explain the striking fact? Well, if I now change my judgement and judge it *right* to see Freya and if I desire to do the right thing then I shall be motivated to see her, given that I now think it is right to see her. Hence, given that I retain a general desire to do the right thing, motivation will reliably follow a change in judgement. Thus the externalist seems to be able to account for the striking fact.

However, Smith thinks that this externalist account gets the psychology of moral agents wrong because the externalist thinks an agent derives his desire for specific things from a general desire. So, for example, we *derive a desire* to see Beth from the general desire to do what is right; and we *derive a desire* to see Freya from the same general desire to do what is right.

The problem is that we think that the moral agent is someone who is motivated by specific *features* of things and not a *general standing desire* to do what is right. For instance, we might think that the good person would desire to help the homeless person because the homeless person is hungry, cold or lonely. The externalist would claim that the good person does not desire to help the homeless person for these reasons but because it is the right thing to do. But Smith claims that this explanation means there is something abnormal about the moral psychology of a good agent. As he put it:

> Good people care *non-derivatively* about honesty, the weal and woe of their children and friends, the well-being of their fellows, people getting what they deserve, justice, equality and the like, *not just one thing* [the general desire to do what is right] … Indeed, commonsense tells us that being so motivated is a *fetish* or moral vice, not the one and only moral virtue.   (1994: 75, emphasis added)

Smith thinks that both the internalist and the externalist would accept the empirical claim that a change in motivation follows reliably in the wake of a change in moral judgement. Furthermore, he thinks that the internalist gives the best explanation of it. The externalist can explain the striking fact but at the price of turning the good person into a *moral fetishist* – someone who is driven by a general non-specific desire to do the right thing. Therefore, Smith claims that we should adopt internalism.

A problem for Smith's argument?

It seems that Smith's characterization of a good moral agent is wrong. We recall he has a problem with the notion of a background general desire to do what is right and believes that this general desire gets the psychology of the good agent wrong. An example from Hallvard Lillehammer appears to challenge Smith's claim:

> Consider … the case of the father who discovers that his son is a murderer, and who knows that if he does not go to the police the boy will get away with it, whereas if he does go to the police the boy will go to the gas-chamber. *The father judges that it is right* to go to the police, and does so … If what moves the father to inform on his son is a *standing [general] desire to do what*

is right …, then this could be as much of a saving grace as a moral failing. Why should it be an *a priori* demand that someone should have an *underived desire* to send his son to death?

(1997: 192, emphasis added)

Perhaps then Smith's argument fails, for in some instances the good agent *might* have a general desire to do what is right. There are also other worries. It seems that the general desire to do what is right needs to be something the agent is consciously aware of for Smith's argument to work. But we might think that this gets the phenomenology of desires wrong. In particular, we can have background desires of which we might not be aware but that influence and change our behaviour. For example, one may have a general desire to be healthy, but not be conscious of it, or a desire to cross the road without ever bringing this to the "front of one's mind". Therefore Smith's argument may depend on an account of desire that does not fit with our everyday understanding.

Perhaps we need to try another approach in order to resolve the debate between internalism and externalism. The debate between internalism and externalism is about the link between judgement and motivation, and another key discussion in moral psychology concerns the *nature* of motivation rather than the nature of this link.

The Humean account of motivation

The Humean account of motivation – an account that Hume himself probably did not hold (Millgram 1995) – is probably the most widely held account of motivation among metaethicists. This is because its main claims are simple, unifying and seem so obviously correct.

Throughout the book we have talked about belief as a *description* of the world. For example, a belief that there is a man on the roof can be characterized as a description *that* there is a man on the roof. However, descriptions seem to be "inert"; speaking metaphorically, they "just sit there". They are sensitive to what the world is like but the belief itself does not try to change the world in any way. For example, if I believe that my bike has two inflated tyres and find out that one is flat my belief will change. There is nothing in having the belief itself that means I will try to change the world so that I have two inflated tyres. If beliefs are descriptions, it is hard to see how a belief *on its own* is going to move us.

What injects the dynamism into belief? A natural answer is that it is only when we *desire* something that the belief will move us. Going back to our example, if I believe I have a flat tyre but desire to go cycling then I shall be motivated to inflate my tyre. Therefore, in contrast to beliefs being sensitive to how the world is, it seems that desires try to get the world to fit them. (This way of distinguishing beliefs from desires is sometimes called the *"direction of fit"* metaphor; see Humberstone 1992.) It is because I desire to go cycling that I shall try to change the world – by inflating my tyre – to accord with my desire. It seems then that if beliefs are going to motivate there will have to be some desires that are appropriately related to those beliefs.

Of course, beliefs do play *some* role. For example, if I want to lose weight but do not believe that exercise can help then I will not be motivated to exercise. So although it seems that desires give us the dynamism, beliefs are required as well. The point, though, is that it seems that while desires are sufficient for motivation, beliefs are only ever necessary.

What we can say then is that intuitively someone is motivated if and only if they have a desire and an appropriately related belief. This is the first part of the Humean theory. The second part is that there is no *necessary* link between beliefs and desires. Beliefs and desires are two distinct mental states. For any case we can think of, where an agent is motivated, the Humean says it is possible that the agent might not have been motivated because he might have lacked a relevant desire.

To summarize, the Humean account of motivation is the most widely accepted, and it claims that in any case where an agent is motivated then that agent will have a desire and an appropriately related belief. Moreover in any case where the agent *is* motivated the agent could have lacked the belief or the desire and failed to be motivated. The account is popular because it fits well with how people think and talk.

Is the Humean account really so obvious?

However plausible the Humean account is, we may wonder whether it can be *universally* true. Can we know *a priori* that any case of motivation will involve a belief and an appropriately related desire? The first challenge has to be to try to find an example where we think motivation is present but where it seems no desire needs to be present. This is not an *argument*, and it will be far too hasty to convince even the most wavering Humean, but looking to such an example will challenge the presumption that the Humean account fits nicely with how we intuitively think and talk.

Consider an example: imagine that you have a wicked stepmother. She purposefully thwarts all your plans; she sabotages your relationship and is generally a nasty piece of work. In a mad moment you promise her that if she was ever ill you would visit her in hospital. To your annoyance she becomes unwell and is rushed into hospital. Given your promise, you begrudgingly commit to visit her once a week (half suspecting that her illness is self-inflicted so as to make a point).

This is a case where you are motivated to do something: to go to the hospital. If the account is right you have a belief and an appropriately related desire. The belief seems easy to identify – you believe that it is the right thing to do because of your promise – but what about your desire? On the face of it we might think that you have *no* relevant desire to see her – after all, you hate the woman. Shafer-Landau puts this point like this:

> [Agents] in such situations often describe their motivations in this way: I wanted to give in, yield to my desires [e.g. the desire *not* to visit the hospital]. I didn't because I thought it would be wrong to do so. I didn't want to *x* (stand in front of that bullet, accept the blame, remain chaste [see my step-mum]), but duty called. I knew what had to be done, and did it, desires (passions, wants, inclinations) be damned.   (2003: 123)

Now of course we speak loosely and our explanations are often incomplete. Furthermore, we may be deceived by the desires we do actually have and consequently our explanations often fail to give all the factors involved. So the Humean might claim that despite this way of talking and explaining, and despite what it feels like to you, there is a desire present in this case.

What is the best response to these sorts of examples? The Humean could argue in some cases that both the way we talk and our phenomenology should take a back seat so that these sorts of cases would not count against them. Or we could take the way we talk and our phenomenology as more important evidence, in which case we might reject the Humean account and think that there could be examples where an agent can be motivated but there is *no desire* present. Shafer-Landau thinks that our interpretative principles give us reason to take the latter option and reject the Humean option. He asks why we should:

> think that all such testimony [from people who do not cite desires as part of their motivation to act] must involve deception: either self-deception, or the intended deception of one's audience? It seems instead that interpretative principles give us reason to render such judgement only as a last resort. Common sense tells us that ordinarily our desires accompany, and often prompt our actions. It also tells us that they sometimes don't.
>
> (*Ibid.*)

There is, then, a conflict here. The Humean gains support for his view by pointing to the fact that people think motivation comprises of beliefs and desires. But, as we have noted, people also talk about cases where they are motivated but lack desire. It seems then that either the Humean uses how people think and talk as evidence and thus leaves their view open to these sorts of counter-examples, or they do not give so much weight to how people think and talk and in so doing lose support for their view.

If one rejects the Humean account, one could argue that moral *beliefs* are sometimes sufficient for motivation and that consequently in these cases there need be no desires at all. One could argue that moral beliefs *necessitate* desires and that this leads to the agent being motivated. Or one could argue that every time someone is motivated there is a desire present, but that this does *not* play a direct role in motivation. Of course, one might even think that the distinction between belief and desires does not capture all the possible mental states and in this vein some philosophers talk about a distinct state called a *besire* (see e.g. Zangwill 2008).

Now that we have introduced internalism, the Humean account and cognitivism we can outline a vital problem regarding their relationship: one that is so important that Michael Smith (1994) calls it *the* moral problem.

The Humean account, internalism and cognitivism: the moral problem

Throughout the book we have talked about the intuitive appeal of three positions: the Humean account, which we have just looked at; the internalist account, which claims that there is a *necessary* link between judgement and motivation; and cognitivism, the view that moral judgements express beliefs. It would be useful if we could retain all three but this is problematic, and in fact metaethicists often argue against one or more of these views by arguing for the other or others. For instance, they might argue that internalism and the Humean account are both correct, and that this shows that we ought to reject cognitivism (in fact, we showed in Chapters 2 and 6 that this was a reason non-cognitivists give in support of their position); or they might argue that cognitivism and the Humean account are both correct and that consequently we should be externalists. It is no surprise, then, that many realists in metaethics – who by virtue of being realists are cognitivists – are also externalists (e.g. Brink 1984; Boyd 1988; Railton 2003). Or there are realists, and therefore cognitivists, who think that internalism is correct and reject the Humean account (e.g. McNaughton 1988; Dancy 1993; McDowell 1998). This inconsistent triad of internalism, the Humean account and cognitivism is a way of understanding the key developments in a lot of metaethics. We shall now consider this inconsistency in more detail.

Cognitivism, yes; the Humean account, yes; internalism, no

Assume that cognitivism is true and that moral judgements express beliefs. So for example, judging that giving money to charity is right is to express the belief that giving money to charity is right. Further, assume that the Humean account of motivation is true. This means that beliefs alone cannot motivate and there cannot be a necessary connection between belief and desire. But holding cognitivism and the Humean account seems to force us to *reject* internalism. If moral judgements express beliefs, and beliefs cannot entail desires, then a moral judgement may or may not be accompanied by a desire. But given we are assuming the desires are necessary for motivation, that means that moral judgements may or may not motivate. But that is to reject internalism, which claims that moral judgements *necessarily* motivate.

The Humean account, yes; internalism, yes; cognitivism, no

Assume that the Humean account is true and that motivation is possible only if there are appropriately related desires and beliefs, and beliefs cannot entail desires. Furthermore, assume that internalism is correct. This means that moral judgements necessarily motivate and thus cannot express beliefs, i.e. cognitivism must be false. For if a judgement is necessarily connected to motivation and beliefs *are not* sufficient to motivate an agent, then judgements cannot be beliefs. They would be expressions of desires (or more generally non-cognitive states).

Internalism, yes; cognitivism, yes; the Humean account, no

Finally, assume that cognitivism is true and that moral judgements express beliefs. Furthermore, assume that internalism is correct and moral judgements necessarily motivate. This means we have to reject the Humean account, which argues that for motivation we need desires and beliefs, so in order for moral judgements that are beliefs to *necessarily motivate* every time someone makes a moral judgement, necessarily there would need to be a desire present. But to ensure this, beliefs would have to entail desires, which is explicitly rejected by the Humean account.

What this apparent inconsistency provides is a possible way of moving on in the seemingly intractable debate between the internalist and externalist. For if these three really are incompatible, then arguing about the Humean account and cognitivism would move us towards a conclusion in the internalist and externalist debate.

Interestingly, some philosophers have argued that it *is* possible to keep all three positions – most notably Michael Smith (1994). Given what we have said, if this works it would be an attractive position.

Conclusion

Some of the most central debates in metaethics concern the agent's psychology. The two that take up the most space in the literature are between internalists and externalists, and Humeans and anti-Humeans. In particular, metaethicists are concerned with what best explains the link between moral judgement and motivation and how to best explain what it is to be motivated.

The centrality of moral psychology is partly due to how it influences other areas of metaethics. For example, if you are an internalist and a Humean then you might be forced to reject cognitivism and, given that realism requires cognitivism, you should reject realism. Consequently, we can see that issues in moral psychology directly affect other areas we have dealt with in this book.

Furthermore, the development and attraction of non-cognitivism is in part traceable to these issues in psychology. Adopting non-cognitivism has the immediate benefit of allowing someone to hold onto the Humean account and internalism (see e.g. Blackburn's argument from practicality, which we discussed in Chapter 6).

Do we want to keep, cognitivism, internalism or the Humean account? Or should we try to follow Smith's example and keep all three?

THINGS TO REMEMBER:

- Internalism about motivation is distinct from internalism about reasons.
- Smith's "striking fact" is an *empirical generalization* and is not meant to be a conceptual truth. Consequently it can be accepted by both internalists and externalists.
- The amoralist is not someone who is nasty or does not want to be moral: she is someone who makes a moral judgement, but is not motivated.
- The debate about motivation is not the same as a debate about action.
- The debate about motivation is independent of whether moral judgements are true or false.
- The Humean account includes the claim that beliefs and desires are distinct mental states; the Humean claims that beliefs never *entail* desires.

Further reading

The *locus classicus* of the debate between internalism and externalism is Smith (1994: ch. 3). A good starting-point in the discussion about both internalism and the Humean account can be found in Shafer-Landau (2003: pt III). The moral problem is first introduced and discussed in Smith (1994: ch. 1). There is a large amount of often complicated literature surrounding these issues. A number of accessible discussions of internalism and externalism are Miller (1996), Smith (1996), Sadler (2003) and Zangwill (2003). For an interesting discussion about how empirical studies in psychology might influence metaethics see Roskies (2003). A good accessible discussion of the Humean account, cognitivism and motivation can be found in Dancy (1993: ch. 1).

9

Moral epistemology

[W]e should think for ourselves, not just listen to our intuitions.

(Singer 2007: 1)

CHAPTER AIMS
- To explain the epistemic regress argument.
- To explain and critically discuss scepticism, intuitionism and coherentism.
- To explain why moral epistemology might matter in areas of metaethics.
- To discuss the role of epistemology within metaethics.

Introduction

I was watching a documentary a number of years ago and was stunned when a suited man recounted the following:

> "I witnessed the whole family being tested on suffocating gas and dying in the gas chamber," … "The parents, son and a daughter. The parents were vomiting and dying, but till the very last moment they tried to save their kids by doing mouth-to-mouth breathing."
> (*This World*, BBC television, 1 February 2004)

What I *knew* then and there was that testing suffocating gas on political prisoners is morally abhorrent. This seemed immediate, involuntary and not inferred. However, moral sceptics argue there are good reasons to think that we *cannot* have any moral knowledge. They would argue that I cannot *know* that testing suffocating gas on political prisoners is morally abhorrent or that the Holocaust was morally wrong or that famine relief is a good thing.

In contrast, other metaethicists are more optimistic about the possibility of moral knowledge. For example, intuitionists and coherentists would argue that moral knowledge is possible. The aim of this chapter is to outline scepticism and these other positions and see how they relate to other metaethical issues. The best way of doing this is to start with the *epistemic regress argument*.

The epistemic regress argument

It seems plausible to claim that to *know* something we must be justified in believing it. For example, if we believe that Spain will win the football World Cup but only believe this because an octopus put a tentacle on Spain's flag, then we would not know that Spain would win the World Cup. Octopus movements do not *justify* belief as to which is the best football team in the world. We need justification for knowledge.

The regress argument starts from the observation that a belief is justified if we have good reason to think that it is true. For example, my belief that we are having curry for dinner is justified if I have a good reason to think this. From this simple point we seem to generate an infinite regress. Consider a tasty example from O'Brien:

> My belief that *the local Asian restaurant is not serving chana puri this week* is justified by my belief that *it is Ramadan*, and my belief that *the breakfast chef does not work during this religious festival*. Thus, belief A [e.g. the local Asian restaurant is not serving chana puri this week] is justified by belief B [e.g. the breakfast chef does not work during this religious festival] and belief C [e.g. that it is Ramadan]. Such justification is inferential: given B and C, I infer that A is true. However, for B and C to play a justifying role, I require further reasons to think that these are true. There is, then, the danger of a regress of justification. Even if belief C is justified by belief D – I believe it is Ramadan because my calendar says so – a question will still arise concerning whether I have good reason to hold this further belief [e.g. that my calendar says so] (and so on). (2006: 61)

It seems then that the beliefs we have gain justification by inference from other beliefs, but these are also beliefs that need justification, and so on. This can seemingly go on *ad infinitum*. Faced with this potential infinite regress we seem to have four options.

(a) Agree that there is an infinite regress in beliefs.
(b) Claim that the regress stops at beliefs but these beliefs are *not* justified (scepticism).
(c) Claim that the regress stops at beliefs and these beliefs are non-inferentially justified (intuitionism).
(d) Claim that the regress stops because some beliefs are justified in virtue of being part of a coherent set of beliefs (coherentism).

Even though there are interesting things to be said in defence of (a) (see Sanford 1984) we shall focus on (b)–(d), starting with scepticism.

Epistemic scepticism: moral beliefs cannot be justified

As the account about gassing prisoners illustrates, scepticism seems false. Surely we *know* it is morally wrong to gas people, just as we know that it is wrong to skin children, instigate mass starvation and so on. However, the sceptic argues that despite our feelings on the matter we are wrong and there is no way of defending the claim that we are justified in our moral beliefs.

One strategy they adopt is to undermine precisely this sense of certainty. The sceptic would argue that even though we take our *feelings* that certain things are right and wrong as evidence that we can *know* these things are right and wrong, we should not. For instance, there is a growing amount of fascinating work that shows that the feelings we take as certain are fickle, and can be manipulated by altering what we would class as philosophically irrelevant factors such as gender, empathy, educational background and timing.

So, for example, if people are told a story where they are asked to save five people or one person (e.g. in the trolley problem), their answers will differ depending on things such as whether the story is told in the first or third person, or told before or after other dilemmas (see e.g. Alexander & Weinberg 2007). As Stacey Swain *et al.* state:

> To the extent that [our beliefs that some things just are right/wrong] are sensitive to these sorts of variables, they are ill-suited

> to do the work philosophers ask of them. [These beliefs] track more than just the philosophically-relevant content of the thought-experiments; they track factors that are irrelevant to the issues the thought-experiments attempt to address. The particular socio-economic status and cultural background of a person who considers a thought experiment should be irrelevant to whether or not that thought-experiment presents a case of knowledge. Such sensitivity to irrelevant factors undermines intuitions' status as evidence. (2008: 141)

Perhaps culture, physical revulsion or the references to family are the elements which lead to our certainty that the gassing of prisoners is wrong. If so, then this seems to threaten the claim that we can just know that some things are either right or wrong.

These points together with the regress argument mean that the sceptic can challenge those who think we can have moral knowledge to give a coherent argument in favour of such a claim.

The intuitionist does this by claiming that we *can* have moral knowledge because some moral beliefs are self-justifying; and the coherentist thinks we can have moral knowledge because beliefs can be justified, since they are part of a coherent set of beliefs.

However, intuitionism – the view that *understanding* some beliefs is sufficient to justify our believing them – seems strange. We might, for example, find it hard to see how understanding that giving money to charity is right justifies us in believing it. If we claim we know that gassing prisoners is wrong but think we do not need to give further reasons for this, then is this not merely stubbornness? We might think that intuitionism is simply a licence for anyone to claim moral knowledge about anything.

What about coherentism – the view that because a belief is part of a coherent set of other beliefs it is justified? Why should this be true? After all, it is unclear why putting a belief that is not justified into a set of beliefs suddenly means it is now justified. Where does the justification spring from?

We shall say a bit more about scepticism before we consider what the intuitionist and coherentist would say to this sort of challenge. The sceptic argues that justification for our moral beliefs is *inferential* and that the line of inference *ends*. However, the last belief in the chain is not justified, and consequently no moral belief is justified. To put it metaphorically: because the last belief is not anchored in justification the chain of belief floats free, unjustified. If this is right then we are never justified in, for example, believing that torturing children is evil, or that charity work is good or that keeping promises is the right thing to do.

A few qualifications and an implication of this sceptical view are required. There is a whole host of philosophical positions called "moral scepticism", such as the view that moral claims are not truth-apt, that moral claims are always false or that there are no good reasons to be moral. However, the scepticism in this chapter is about *justification*: it is the claim that no moral beliefs are justified.

Furthermore, there need be *no* direct practical implication of accepting moral scepticism. As one of the most prominent moral sceptics, Walter Sinnott-Armstrong, states:

> [Moral sceptics] need not be any less motivated to be moral, nor need they have any less reason to be moral, than their opponents. Moral skeptics can hold moral beliefs just as strongly as nonskeptics. Moral skeptics can even believe that their moral beliefs are true by virtue of corresponding to an independent reality. All that moral skeptics must deny is that their (or anyone's) moral beliefs are *justified* in the relevant way, but this is enough to make moral skepticism very controversial and important. (2006: 8)

One of the reasons that *this* scepticism about justification is important is because of its implications for other areas of metaethics. For instance, it has direct relevance to the debate about realism (see Chapters 4 and 5). Let us briefly consider why.

One reason for adopting moral realism might be that moral properties mean we *can have* moral knowledge. If killing, as a matter of fact, has the property of being wrong then we can potentially come to know this. However, if moral scepticism is correct then we cannot have knowledge and, in particular, we cannot know that killing has the property of wrongness. Realism might seem much less attractive if scepticism were correct and consequently we could never be justified in our moral beliefs. In fact epistemology is often a reason why realism is rejected: "Many of those who are sceptical of moral realism are sceptical on epistemological grounds" (*ibid.*: 100).

Even given the worries about trying to give a response to the regress argument through intuitionism and coherentism, it seems that if the only other option is to adopt scepticism then we should try harder to respond to these worries. We shall start with intuitionism (c), the claim that some beliefs are *non-inferentially* justified.

If intuitionism is right, how do we acquire moral knowledge?

One thing that makes the literature on moral epistemology hard to understand is that the term "intuitionism" is often used in two different ways. Sometimes it is used to describe a worked out *moral theory* but on other occasions it is used as a claim about how moral beliefs are justified. Of course, we can combine these so that we might defend intuitionism-the-theory via the claim that by understanding some moral beliefs we are justified in believing them (see e.g. Ross 1930). But these views are distinct, and we shall ignore the moral theory and stick to intuitionism as a claim about *epistemic justification*.

Intuitionism holds that we can respond to the sceptic by claiming that the regress stops with moral beliefs that are non-inferentially justified. As suggested in the gassing of prisoners example, intuitionism seems to ring true with what it is like to be moral; it seems to fit with the phenomenology of being a moral agent. So can the intuitionists tell us more?

Intuitionism: moral knowledge through moral observation

The first question we might have is: by what mechanism, or by what faculty, can we come to have these non-inferentially justified beliefs? Intuitionists typically have two answers; the first focuses on *a posteriori* knowledge and the second *a priori* knowledge. We shall consider these options in turn.

If you look at the sky, are you justified in believing that it is blue? Or looking at this page, are you justified in your belief that there are words on it? In most cases you think you *are* but on reflection it does not seem that such beliefs are justified through an inference from other beliefs. You just focused your eyes in a particular place and looked. Observation seems to show that we can come to know certain things but this knowledge is *not* based on inferential justification.

But can an appeal to observation really help? After all, we are inter-ested in *moral* knowledge, and is not moral observation a little odd? Everyday observations such as seeing that my bike is dirty or that the front door is open seem nothing like our experience of arriving at moral beliefs. How should we understand the notion of "moral observation"?

If we think that observation is limited to these sorts of cases – cases where there are mind-independent things with which we come into cognitive contact through our five senses – then moral observation will be a strange view. For we do not experience moral properties in this way: we do not see wrongness floating over a stabbing or peek-ing out from a wallet being stolen. However, as McNaughton (1988) writes:

> We might suppose that the only properties that can be observed are the "proper objects" of the five senses: touch, shape, and texture; hearing, sound, and so on. If we adopt this austere account of what can be perceived it is clear that not only moral properties but a great many of the things we normally take ourselves to perceive will be, strictly speaking, unobservable. *If, on the other hand, we are prepared to allow that I can see that this cliff is dangerous, that Smith is worried, or that one thing is further away than another, then there seems no reason to be squeamish about letting in moral observation.*
>
> (1988: 57, emphasis added)

Although this is a promising way of proceeding, we might put pressure on the claim that moral observation gives us non-inferential beliefs by noting that it seems that moral observation only takes place against a background of other beliefs. For example, it might be because you hold a certain moral theory that you observe the wrongness of a situation.

However, this would only be the start of an argument against intui-tionism. To threaten intuitionism further we would have to show that our moral observations are not only made by people with a whole host of other beliefs but also that the beliefs gained through moral observa-tions obtain their justification by virtue of some of those beliefs. For example, when we form the belief that there are clouds in the sky we might also have other beliefs about the sky being blue, about the time of day, about what we are going to have for dinner and so on, but these beliefs do not justify the belief that there are clouds in the sky. Some may be relevant and some may be irrelevant but that is not the same as them being used to justify the belief that there are clouds in the sky.

Therefore the intuitionist can admit that other moral beliefs *are* present when we make a moral observation and that we do not form non-inferential moral beliefs in isolation, but at the same time claim that these beliefs are not used as inferential justification. Perhaps thinking hard about what it is for one belief to justify another belief can help moral intuitionists when employing the idea of moral observation.

Intuitionism: moral knowledge through *a priori* reflection

We might think that talk of moral observation will be limited in the following ways. Talk of observation seems out of place for many of our moral beliefs and in particular for future or hypothetical situations. Furthermore, moral observation seems only capable of giving us specific verdicts. I observe the wrongness of this or that case. How could observation give us knowledge of general claims such as that torture is always wrong? (Some theorists would deny we can have such general knowledge; e.g. Ridge & McKeever 2008.)

Arguably the intuitionist's analogy with *a priori* knowledge can help to deal with these sorts of worries, through the claim that by reasoning and reflection we can acquire moral beliefs that are non-inferentially justified.

Key to this view is the idea that some moral beliefs are *self-evident*. Here is a famous quotation concerning the kinds of moral beliefs that might be considered so: "We hold these truths to be self-evident, that all men are created equal, that they are endowed by their Creator with certain unalienable Rights, that among these are Life, Liberty and the pursuit of Happiness" (US Declaration of Independence). Or, slightly less famously, Shafer-Landau states:

> It seems to me self-evident that, other things being equal, it is wrong to take pleasure in another's pain, to taunt and threaten the vulnerable, to prosecute and punish those known to be innocent, and to sell another's secrets solely for personal gain.
> (2003: 248)

Of course, these may not be genuine self-evident beliefs. The general idea, though, is that *if* they are, then understanding them is enough to justify us in believing them. Based on the work of Robert Audi (1998) let us now clear up a number of misconceptions about self-evidence and with it a number of worries that people have about this form of *a priori* intuitionism.

(a) *Self-evidence does not entail infallibility.* Although it may be true that we have a self-evident moral belief, this may not be obvious to us. There is nothing in the notion of a self-evident moral belief that means that if we think we have one we do. Crucially, then, an intuitionist cannot claim to have a monopoly on moral knowledge because he cannot be sure that the beliefs he thinks are self-evident actually are.

(b) *We can change our mind about what is self-evident.* Let us grant that we understand and accept a self-evident belief on the basis of this understanding. This does not mean that it forces us to hold onto it at all costs. For instance, if it *is* a self-evident belief that racism is wrong and we understand it and accept it on the basis of understanding it, we know it. However, we could at some point change our views on the issue.

(c) *Self-evidence does not rule out inferential justification.* We could understand a moral belief and come to accept it because we understand it. This would mean we know it. However this does not rule out the possibility of giving reasons why it is we came to recognize it as true. The point is that when we have a self-evident belief then, if we understand it and believe it, on that basis we are justified in believing it. As long as *this* is in place we can also talk about reasons and inferences and explanations and this will not undermine intuitionism.

With these qualifications, we can see how intuitionism can begin to respond to a number of common charges against it.

First, people might charge intuitionists with being arrogant. If an intuitionist believes that racism is morally acceptable then she might claim that she understands this and accepts it on that basis; consequently, she might conclude that she *knows* racism is acceptable. Is intuitionism a licence for anyone to assert that he or she *knows* any moral claim they choose to accept? No, because we can be wrong about what we think are self-evident beliefs. So in our example, the racist cannot know whether his beliefs about racism are self-evident. Therefore, even if intuitionism is true, we should still be circumspect in holding that we know this or that moral claim.

Second, you can be an intuitionist and a naturalist. It is true that a number of prominent intuitionists such as Moore ([1903] 1993) were non-naturalists, but we do not need to adopt a particular view on the nature of moral properties. We cannot then argue from the supposed implausibility of non-naturalism to the falsity of intuitionism.

Third is the concern that the intuitionist requires some kind of special faculty that allows people to acquire non-inferentially justified beliefs. So, for example, Mackie thinks intuitionism should be rejected because it requires: "some *special faculty … utterly different from our ordinary way of knowing everything else*" (1977: 39, emphasis added). Mackie does not develop this claim but given what we have said about *a posteriori* and *a priori* knowledge, what he says seems mistaken. For arguably there is no special faculty required when we acquire non-inferentially justified beliefs through *observation* and *reflection*.

What these qualifications have shown is that both *a priori* intuitionism and *a posteriori* intuitionism are more resilient than we might initially have thought. We shall now briefly consider how plausible it is to accept the coherentist's claim that some beliefs are justified because they are part of a coherent set of beliefs.

An introduction to coherentism

The coherentist argues that moral knowledge is possible. The basic idea is that a moral belief will be justified if it relates in the right way to the right set of coherent beliefs. As Geoffrey Sayre-McCord writes:

> What matters to her coherentism, as I see it, is that she thinks (negatively) that there is no epistemologically privileged class of beliefs and (positively) that beliefs are justified only if, and then to the extent that, they cohere well with the other beliefs one holds. (1996: 152)

We might think this idea of coherence seems a bit suspicious. Is it not somehow circular? I have heard people say they believe in God because the Bible says he exists and the Bible is the inspired word of God. Clearly this does not give us justification for God existing because the reasoning is circular. But if the coherentist's idea is that the beliefs gain justification because they circle back on themselves, then why is this any different?

The answer is that the type of justification that the coherence account relies on is different. The circular reasoning in the Bible and God example relies on a *linear* form of justification. One belief is justified by another, which is justified by another, which is justified by another and eventually the beliefs circle back on themselves. However, the coherentist relies on a *holistic* account of justification. The oft-cited metaphor is that of a raft. A raft stays afloat not because of a particular plank (belief) but because of how the whole structure hangs together (whole set of coherent beliefs). Because of this holistic account of justification the coherentist can talk about a belief being justified without the charge of circularity. The fundamental unit of evaluation when it comes to epistemic justification is the whole of the system of beliefs an agent has. A belief – say, that giving to charity is the right thing to do – is justified if and only if it is part of the most coherent set available.

The plausibility of this account will rely on the requirements for something to be coherent. We shall make some general comments that are loosely based on the work of Sayre-McCord (1996).

The first requirement for a set of beliefs to be coherent is that the set must be *logically* consistent. We cannot have a coherent set that contains a belief and its negation. For example, I cannot believe that Grace is Jon's daughter and also believe that it is not the case that Grace is Jon's daughter.

The second requirement is that the belief must be *evidentially* consistent. Imagine I believe both that it is highly unlikely that Matt will win the lottery and that Matt has won the lottery. This *is* logically consistent, but we might still think it is not coherent, because "the weight of the evidence provided by the various beliefs [it is highly unlikely that Matt will win the lottery and Matt has won the lottery] … in the set … tell, on balance, against … others" (1996: 166).

However, evidential and logical consistency are not enough. We can imagine sets of beliefs that lack coherence but which are nevertheless evidentially and logically consistent. For example, imagine we have three beliefs: it is raining; Freya and Beth are beautiful; spiders hear with their feet. This is certainly logically consistent and evidentially consistent but we might not think it is particularly coherent, because the beliefs are about *unrelated* things.

In contrast, if we consider a set of beliefs that are about the same things and are logically and evidentially consistent, then we will want to say that the set is *coherent*. Imagine that I believe it is always sunny in South Carolina, that Tim is in South Carolina and that the sun is shining on Tim. This seems coherent, for not only is it evidentially consistent and logically consistent but it also has *connectedness*. The beliefs are related to one another, and one of the beliefs can be inferred from the others. So although consistency is good for coherence, if the evidence in support of the beliefs support each other then it is even better.

Yet there may still be a concern that coherence is too easy to come by, for there might be only *two* beliefs in a set that would be coherent because it is logically consistent and evidentially consistent and has connectedness. Thus the *size* of the set of beliefs is important. If we have two sets of beliefs that are equally consistent and equally connected but one has more beliefs in it, then that one is more coherent. So whether a set of beliefs is coherent will involve considerations of logical consistency, evidential consistency, connectedness and size.

The coherentist's response to the sceptic then is that we can have moral knowledge, since our moral beliefs can be justified because they are part of a coherent set of beliefs. This hardly scratches the surface in a discussion about how best to construct coherence. However, rather than getting into this we shall outline a concern about coherentism.

A worry about coherentism

We might think that in some important way justification should be related to the world. However, if the coherence account is correct then it does not seem to be. Consider an example. In 1988 a 65-year-old Polish railway worker, Jan Grzebski, fell into a coma after he was hit by a train. In 2007 he woke and said:

> When I went into a coma there was only tea and vinegar in the shops, meat was rationed and huge petrol queues were everywhere … Now I see people on the streets with mobile phones and there are so many goods in the shops it makes my head spin.
> (BBC 2007)

If we assume that in 1988 Jan's beliefs were justified because they were part of a coherent set, then this would mean that as he woke from his coma in 2007 his beliefs would still be justified. Obviously he would form more beliefs when he realized it was 2007 and that he had been in a coma, but this would not be the *same* set of beliefs. However, if he continued to have the same beliefs he had in 1988 then according to the coherentist he would continue to be *justified*.

This might seem strange and one reason for this is that justification seems somehow to be related to *truth*: for example, if our belief that killing is wrong is *justified* because it is part of the most *coherent* set of beliefs, then we might think that being part of the most coherent set of beliefs means my belief is *more likely* to be true. As Laurence Bonjour states:

> one crucial part of the task of an adequate epistemological theory is to show that there is an appropriate connection between its proposed account of epistemic justification and the cognitive goal of truth. That is, it must somehow be shown that justification as conceived by the theory is *truth-conducive*, that one who seeks justified beliefs is at least likely to find true ones. (1988: 108–9, emphasis added)

The problem is that if you consider the criteria for coherence it does not mention *truth*. So it is possible on the coherentist account of justification for a coherent set of beliefs to be mainly false. The coherentist is therefore seemingly forced to accept that we can have a belief that is justified but may *not* be true. For example, if our belief that killing is wrong is justified because it is part of the most *coherent* set of beliefs then this does not mean that the belief that killing is wrong is *more likely* to be true.

It is because of these difficulties that some coherentists have been keen to argue for both a coherence theory of justification and a coherence theory of truth (*ibid.*). We do not need to go into the details of such an account here, but note that if the coherence theory of *truth* is correct then we cannot have a coherent set that is mainly false. This in turn means that justification *can* be thought as *truth*-conducive and one of the main arguments against coherentism can be met.

Conclusion

Surely we can *know* that testing suffocating gas on families is wrong and it is hard to believe that any person could doubt that fact. However, philosophers have questioned whether we can be so confident about this. The sceptic, relying on the epistemic regress argument and the problems with intuitionism and coherentism, forces us to give a philosophical defence of moral knowledge. The intuitionist thinks that we can be justified in believing a moral belief in virtue of understanding it. The coherentist thinks that moral beliefs are justified by being part of a coherent set of beliefs.

Irrespective of which position we decide to adopt, there is a general methodological question worth thinking about. A student of mine summed this up in an email:

> The problems we covered for moral epistemology were mostly general epistemological issues, and people are still trying to solve them in that field. … *So do you not think it would be wise to just leave moral epistemology*, and see what the general fallout is from people looking at these issues in straight epistemology, and then the conclusions can be applied to Metaethics?
>
> (Edward Costelloe, pers. comm.)

This is a good question. Should we wait for the epistemologists to come to conclusions and transplant these into the metaethical domain? Or ought we to think about moral knowledge independently from other general debates in epistemology? We need to decide where to put our efforts. Does solving the epistemological concerns mean we can draw conclusions about ontology, psychology or language? If "many of those who are sceptical of moral realism are sceptical on epistemological grounds" then if we can sort out the epistemology this might leave the way open to adopting realism. Or should the ontology take centre stage and once we choose realism, anti-realism or whatever, we can decide which epistemology fits best? Moreover, we might believe that there are some unique issues that can only be discussed and thought about from within metaethics, and that we cannot simply transplant issues without qualification from other areas. Perhaps issues to do with normativity mean that we cannot think about epistemology, ontology, psychology or language apart from ethics? However, whatever we decide, it seems that issues in epistemology are going to have an influence on what is and is not attractive to us within the rest of metaethics.

THINGS TO REMEMBER

- Intuitionism can refer to a moral theory or an account of epistemic justification.
- Moral scepticism is not the same as non-cognitivism or a general scepticism about being moral.
- Coherentists reject linear forms of justification so it is unhelpful to characterize them as thinking that moral beliefs "circle back on themselves".
- The intuitionist is not committed to there being non-natural properties.
- Intuitionism does not mean that someone can claim they *know* what things are right and wrong. It is the claim that it is possible to have moral knowledge.

Further reading

O'Brien (2006) is an excellent introduction to general issues in epistemology. Shafer-Landau (2003: pt V) gives a good outline of key positions in moral epistemology and defends an intuitionist position. The *locus classicus* for a coherentist account in moral epistemology is the fascinating but tough paper by Sayre-McCord (1996), and for coherentism in general is Bonjour (1988). A comprehensive and accessible survey of moral scepticism can be found in Sinnott-Armstrong (2006). Two recent papers that defend moral knowledge through perception are Chappell (2008) and Cullison (2010).

10

Fictionalism and non-descriptive cognitivism

It is one thing to show a man that he is in an error, and another to put him in possession of truth.   (John Locke [1690] 1975: bk IV, ch. 7, §11)

We are all pretending the important thing is to keep a straight face.
                                                          (Maurice Valency)

CHAPTER AIMS

- To distinguish hermeneutic fictionalism from revolutionary fictionalism.
- To raise some worries for both forms of fictionalism.
- To outline and criticize cognitive non-descriptivism.

Hermeneutic and revolutionary fictionalism

It is a mistake to think of fictionalism as *one* theory that can be split into hermeneutic and revolutionary views; it is better to think of hermeneutic and revolutionary fictionalism as distinct positions.

Hermeneutic fictionalism is a *descriptive* theory that makes a claim about what our moral practice is like. *Revolutionary* fictionalism is a *prescriptive* theory that makes a claim about what our moral practice ought to be like. With this in mind, it is worth considering the following questions when thinking about each theory.

Hermeneutic fictionalism:
- Is its description of our moral practice accurate?
- Could its description be right even if we do not recognize it as such?

Revolutionary fictionalism:
- Is it true that we ought to change our moral practice?
- Is it possible to change our moral practice?

Hermeneutic fictionalism

Hermeneutic fictionalists argue that even though most people do not ever recognize it, there are good reasons to think that our moral practice is based on make-believe and that we are involved in a moral fiction. They believe, for example, that when in everyday talk we say "giving money to charity is right", we do not actually *believe* that giving money to charity is right, but instead we *make-believe* it. To see why this might be a useful way to think of our moral practice we shall consider another example.

Consider games played by children. My daughters play a game in which they pretend to be Violet and Sunny in an adventure from Lemony Snicket's *A Series of Unfortunate Events*. The chair covered in a blanket is a cave and the stairs are a cliff-face.

In games of make-believe such as this there are rules. In my daughters' game you cannot join in and start doing anything you want. Sunny cannot turn into a robot; Violet cannot row the boat up the cliff and the evil Count Olaf cannot suddenly become a saint. It is also possible to have a meaningful discussion and a disagreement within the game. Once they are playing the game, they can meaningfully ask such questions as "What is the best way to cross the lake?", "Has Count Olaf really left the cave?" and "Is Sunny a better climber than Violet?"

Furthermore, once we are playing a game of make-believe certain things are true or false *within* the game. Continuing our example, it is true that Sunny is a baby, false that Violet can fly, true that Count Olaf is lurking in the cave, true that the cliff-face is dangerous and so on.

What is crucial is that even though these fictional claims *can* be true, no one thinks they are *literally* true. The truth of a claim within a game does not commit us to the existence of the world described. To put it in terms we discussed in Chapter 4, truth in a game of make-believe does not require the truth-*maker* thesis. Although it is true that the cliff-face is snowy, this does not mean we have to go out and buy crampons to get up the stairs. If the hermeneutic fictionalist is right then she can make the following claims about our moral practice.

(a) Moral claims can be true according to the moral fiction.
(b) Moral claims can be true even if there are no moral properties or facts.
(c) We can assert, negate, embed and debate moral claims.

It would be very attractive to be able to accept this set of claims. For if (a) is correct then we can reject error theory (Chapter 3), and if (b) is correct then we can avoid awkward ontological questions about what moral properties and facts are, how we come to know about them and how they relate to non-moral properties and facts (Chapters 4 and 5). However, when we reflect on our own moral practice it does not feel like a fiction and this is a difficulty for the hermeneutic fictionalists.

A challenge to hermeneutic fictionalism: first-person authority

Consider two quotations: "If the hermeneutic fictionalist is correct … this introduces a novel and quite *drastic form of failure of first-person authority* over one's own mental states" (Stanley 2001: 47, emphasis added); and "morality is above all a place where we do not make-believe. We stand fast, thump the table, and find our voices vibrant with conviction" (Blackburn 2005: 9).

An obvious problem with hermeneutic fictionalism is that it claims that our current moral practice is a fiction; yet, when we reflect on it, this does not seem to be the case. For example, when we shout at the television: "but racism is wrong!", our voice is "*vibrant with conviction*"; and when people make life-threatening decisions such as to fight for their country, they do not believe their moral duty is a fiction. Being moral definitely does not *feel* like a fiction! However, it still might be, and it may be possible for us to come to understand why this is the case.

Consider an example that illustrates this possibility. When you comment to your friend that you do not think much of the new crop of students, you have to laugh when he asks you how you farm a field of students. Clearly your statement about it being a "crop of students" was not a literal truth. However, and this is the key, it did not feel any different when it was said.

The reason for this is perhaps that we are so familiar with metaphors that we use them without giving them a second thought. The hermeneutic fictionalist suggests that, in a similar way, we are so familiar with using moral language as a fiction that there is no accompanying phenomenology. This then would be a response to the challenge from first-person authority.

However, although this addresses the basic phenomenological worry, it does lead to a further issue. If there is no way of telling "from the inside" whether we are engaged in make-believe, then how can anyone say with confidence that they are *not* involved in make-believe? In particular, what allows the hermeneutic fictionalist to hold that morality is a fiction but that talk of love, maths, science, history, time or anything else is not?

The obvious way would be to give the speaker authority on the matter so that if *they* say they are not involved in a fiction, then they are not. However, this undermines the response to the phenomenological point.

If there were a test that could provide evidence that morality *is* a fiction while other subjects are not, then this would certainly give credence to the hermeneutic fictionalist's claim. Here is one way we might show this:

Consider a quotation from *The Curious Incident of the Dog in the Night-Time*, an account from the perspective of an autistic child:

> The word "metaphor" means carrying something from one place to another … and it is when you describe something by using a word for something that it isn't. This means that the word "metaphor" is a metaphor. *I think it should be called a lie* because a pig is not like a day and people do not have skeletons in their cupboards. And when I try and make a picture of the phrase in my head *it just confuses me* because imagining an apple in someone's eye doesn't have anything to do with liking someone a lot and it makes you forget what the person was talking about. (Haddon 2004: 20)

This story reflects a truth about autism, namely that people with autism find it hard to deal with fiction, make-believe and pretence. Perhaps we can use this fact as a test? If the hermeneutic fictionalist is right and morality is a fiction, we would expect autistic people to struggle with it in the *same* sort of way as they struggle with other fictions. The problem for the hermeneutic fictionalist is that most empirical studies in psychology conclude that they do not, and consequently our test to help the hermeneutic fictionalist to show that morality is a fiction has failed (see e.g. Wolfberg 1999).

Revolutionary fictionalism

> There is nothing wrong in change, if it is in the right direction. (Winston Churchill, 23 June 1925)

If you are going to have a revolution, you had better have a reason. The revolutionary fictionalist typically takes this reason to be that all our moral judgements are systematically and uniformly *false* and that making false claims is not as beneficial to us as to start engaging in moral fiction.

To understand revolutionary fictionalism better it is worth comparing it to hermeneutic fictionalism. In particular, it is worth considering their different descriptions of our *current* moral practice. To understand this let us consider an example.

Imagine on the one hand a history teacher reading from Tolkien's *The Hobbit* as if it is authentic and on the other an English teacher reading from *The Hobbit* as a fantasy. Arguably we believe that the history teacher is making *false* claims, not the English teacher.

The revolutionary fictionalist argues that currently when we make moral claims we are like the history teacher reading from *The Hobbit* as if it were a true account. The hermeneutic fictionalist would argue that currently when we make moral claims we are like the English teacher: we are entering into a fiction. So the revolutionary fictionalist thinks that we genuinely believe what we are saying when we make moral claims and that consequently when we make a moral claim we are saying something which is false. The hermeneutic fictionalist thinks that we do not actually believe what we are saying when we make moral claims and that consequently our moral talk is not systematically and uniformly false (it is not an error theory). Let us grant with the revolutionary fictionalist that we are all systematically and uniformly false in our moral claims. According to revolutionary fictionalism, we have two options.

(a) We could abandon moral talk altogether – what philosophers call *eliminativism*.
(b) We could agree that all moral talk is systematically and uniformly false, stop believing what we say and start pretending (*revolutionary fictionalism*).

In order for revolutionary fictionalism to be plausible (b) has to be preferable to (a): that is, the revolutionary fictionalist needs to show that it is more beneficial to engage in a fiction than to give up on morality altogether. Drawing on the work of the revolutionary fictionalist Richard Joyce (e.g. 2001, 2005) we shall briefly examine why they think this.

Why not give up being moral?

We might think that if revolutionary fictionalists are right and that all our moral talk is systematically and uniformly false (error theory) then the best thing to do is to abandon our moral talk altogether. Would it not be rather perverse to carry on using moral language when there is nothing answering to it? Consider an example.

Imagine that all the influential astronomers of the day told us live on television that it had now been established that Mars does not actually exist and that the reason we all thought it did was because of some faulty maths and equipment. Every time people talked about Mars, they would be in error. What would happen to our "Mars" talk? Presumably it would drop out of use and, apart from people sometimes talking about how we used to think of Mars as the red planet and so on, people would eventually stop talking about Mars as if it existed.

If this is right, then plausibly the correct response to error theory is (a): eliminativism. If there is no good, bad, evil, right or wrong, and consequently we are in error every time we talk as if there is, then it seems preferable to stop talking about good, bad, evil, right, wrong and so on.

However, among those who think that error theory is correct, only a few have been bold enough to take this route (e.g. Garner 2007). It would certainly be brave for a metaethicist to prescribe that we abandon moral talk altogether. However, the main reason that eliminativism has not been adopted is that metaethicists have argued that something would be lost if people ceased all moral talk.

What would the world be like without moral talk? It is unlikely that we would have anarchy. Presumably people could still be able to coordinate action, instigate rules and punishments and so on without moral talk. So whatever benefit the revolutionary fictionalist identifies, it must be more than simply the ability to coordinate action and so on.

According to Joyce (e.g. 2005), what would be lost is the ease with which we can coordinate action. Morality makes such agreement and coordination easier because such terms as "oughts", "duties" and "obligations" have a certain *gravitas*. If we put rules in moral language then they appear to be beyond negotiation. We seem more able to resist being sidetracked by temptation if issues are couched in moral terms. As Greg Restall *et al.* put it:

> An agent engaging in the pretence that a certain course of action is the right one – an action that "simply must be done" – is more likely to withstand the temptation of doing otherwise, than an agent who simply judges it to be in her best interests to perform it … One might also think that moral vocabulary is required in childrearing. Concepts such as right and wrong, good and bad, virtue and vice might play an indispensable role encouraging children to behave in certain ways, and to refrain from behaving in others. (2005: 314)

Is this the reason that fictionalism would be beneficial over eliminativism? It cannot be. If what we have said so far is correct then all we will have shown is that *believing* in morality is more beneficial than giving it up. If fictionalism is to be plausible we need to show that *make-believing* in morality is more beneficial than giving it up. As Joyce puts it: "The fictionalist wins the argument if she shows that there is *some* benefit to be had from keeping moral discourse as a fiction that would be lost (with no compensating gain) by eliminating moral discourse entirely" (2005: 302, emphasis added).The revolutionary fictionalist argues that this is possible, for it seems that there *are* benefits to be had from engaging in make-believe.

Consider a phenomenon that illustrates the benefits of engaging in make-believe. Emergency room doctors report that over the past twenty years more people than ever are surviving being shot. The explanation is that when people are shot they tend to react in the way they see characters in films react. Given that characters in films are often superhuman in how they cope with gunshot wounds, people will as part of this make-believe think they can survive more than they – physiologically speaking – should. Make-believe in this situation has a direct practical benefit. Joyce gives another example of the benefit of make-believe:

> Suppose I am determined to exercise regularly after a lifetime of lethargy, but find myself succumbing to temptation.

> An effective strategy will be for me to lay down a strong and authoritative rule: *I must do fifty sit-ups every day, no less* ... Perhaps in truth it doesn't much matter that I do fifty sit-ups every day, so long as I do more-or-less fifty on most days. But by allowing myself the occasional lapse, by giving myself permission *sometimes* to stray from the routine ... I threaten even my doing more-or-less fifty sit-ups on most days. I do better if I encourage myself to think in terms of fifty daily sit-ups as a non-negotiable value, as something I *must* do if I am ever to get fit.   (*Ibid.*: 303, emphasis added)

The argument then would be that *make-believing* some actions are right or wrong increases our self-control and consequently we are likely to gain some benefit from engaging in a fiction, compared to giving up morality altogether.

The revolutionary fictionalist is not committed to the implausible claim that we wait until we are tempted to steal, cheat or break a promise before engaging in make-believe about morality. Rather, the suggestion is that when these temptations arise we can resist them because we have already committed ourselves – what Joyce calls a *pre-commitment* – to adopting pretence towards morality. The idea is that given the truth of error theory, we ought to choose to be fictionalists about morality. This means that in any moral situation in the future we shall be guided in a way that will benefit us more than if we had given up morality altogether.

Some worries for revolutionary fictionalism

Imagine people committing themselves to adopting the fictional morality and parents passing this habit on from generation to generation, so:

> a person is simply brought up to think in moral terms; the pre-commitment is put in place by parents. In childhood such prescriptions may be presented and accepted as items of belief ... thus thinking of certain types of action as "morally right" and others as "morally wrong" becomes *natural and ingrained*.
>   (*Ibid.*: 307, emphasis added)

It will be so natural and ingrained that "What goes through ... [the agent's mind] may be exactly the same as what goes through the mind of the sincere moral believer – it need not 'feel' like make-believe at all (and thus it may have the same influence on behaviour as a belief)" (*ibid.*: 306).

The first question we might have is: if this is all true, then how do we know that we have not already had the revolution that revolutionary fictionalists want? In other words, what makes the revolutionary fictionalist so confident that error theory and not hermeneutic fictionalism is the best description of our current moral practice?

Presumably the answer they would give is that at present we are not *pretending* to believe but rather *genuinely* believe that things are right and wrong. Yet we do not want to know how revolutionary fictionalists describe morality as it is, but what justifies their describing it in this way. To put this in another way, the revolutionary fictionalists need to make clear what the difference is between believing that "killing is wrong" and make-believing that "killing is wrong", so that they can identify current practice as believing – rather than make-believing – and can prescribe their revolution. But what can this marker be? It cannot be anything in the minds of people because even make-believe need not feel like make-believe at all. One possible way of responding is that the "difference between the two need only be a disposition that the fictionalist has (though is not paying attention to): the disposition to deny that anything is really morally wrong, when placed in her most critical context [e.g. the philosophy classroom]" (*ibid.*: 306).

We wanted a way of distinguishing both the hermeneutic and the revolutionary description of our current practice. Presumably fictionalists of *both* camps would be disposed to deny that anything is really morally wrong, right and so on. So the theories are still not separated. Given this, further questions need to be asked about the comparison to eliminativism and the normative implication of both revolutionary and hermeneutic fictionalism.

Non-descriptive cognitivism

To finish this chapter it is worth noting a position developed by Horgan and Timmons (e.g. 2000, 2006). It is an important view because it challenges a central assumption we have held throughout this book and also opens up new conceptual space that the metaethicist can explore. We shall outline why they argue that metaethicists have been labouring under a false assumption.

Until now, we have been assuming that if a moral judgement expresses a belief then that moral judgement can be thought of as a description. We have taken cognitivism to be interchangeable with descriptivism.

Horgan and Timmons think that this is a mistake and that, as cognitivists, there is good evidence to accept that moral judgements are expressions of *beliefs*, but that it is best to think of those beliefs expressed by moral judgements as *non-descriptive*. Thus Horgan and Timmons conclude that moral judgements are expressions of non-descriptive beliefs. For example, to claim that killing is wrong is to express a belief, but this is not to describe killing as having the property of wrongness. As they say:

> moral thought and discourse … are not in the business of *representing* or *reporting* moral facts (whether objectively real, constructed, or relative); moral terms and the concepts they express do not function to pick out moral properties. In short, moral judgments are not a species of *descriptive* beliefs. But … we do maintain nonetheless that these judgments are indeed *beliefs*; we reject the view that all beliefs are descriptive beliefs. (2006: 223)

As we shall see, the immediate benefit of this is that it supports the cognitivist nature of our moral practice: it rejects realism but crucially it is not an error theory. This combination is possible because according to Horgan and Timmons beliefs are not describing the world as having any moral properties or facts. Therefore the fact that there are *no* properties or facts does not mean that moral judgements are all false. However, they need to give us some reason for thinking that there are *both* descriptive and non-descriptive beliefs; before we consider this, though, we need to know what they think a belief is.

For Horgan and Timmons, a belief is a psychological commitment to some possible state of affairs. Therefore if there are two types of belief it must be possible to identify two types of commitment. Horgan and Timmons identify these as "*is*-commitments" and "*ought*-commitments". Our everyday non-moral beliefs are is-commitments towards various possible states of affairs, while a moral belief is an ought-commitment towards a possible state of affairs: thus moral judgements express a commitment to what *ought* to be the case.

Granted that this is a feasible and defensible distinction, there are two clear things that Horgan and Timmons need to do. They need to show first why we should think that ought-commitments are beliefs, and second why ought-commitments should be thought of as non-descriptive. If they can accomplish this they will have shown that cognitivist non-descriptivism is a genuine option in metaethics.

Ought-commitments as beliefs

Horgan and Timmons employ a straightforward method to show that moral judgements express beliefs. They identify the characteristics of non-moral judgements by which we express beliefs and then show that moral judgements share these characteristics. They then conclude that given the similarities they are entitled to claim that ought-commitments are beliefs.

Horgan and Timmons (2006) identify three main areas as the characteristics of belief. The first is grammatical, the second is logical and the third is experiential.

Horgan and Timmons identify the following in the first and second features. They say that when we make non-moral judgements we are *declaring* something; we can *negate* non-moral claims, *conjoin* them and perform various other operations on them such as embedding them in conditionals. So, for example, when we judge that "It's raining outside" we are declaring something; we can say "It is *not* the case that it's raining outside", or "It's raining outside *or* it is snowing", or "If it's raining outside then I had better run to my next class". These are some of the logical and grammatical features of non-moral beliefs and they seem to have exactly the same logical and grammatical trappings as *moral* beliefs. When making a moral claim we are declaring something, we can negate, conjoin, and embed them. As Horgan and Timmons write regarding *both* is- and ought-commitments:

> the contents of [both is- and ought-commitments] are *declarative*, and they can figure as constituents in logically complex judgments as in "Either John has paid what he owes to Mary or he *ought* to do so." As such, ought-commitments can figure

in *logical inferences*. Furthermore, they can *combine* with other beliefs to yield new beliefs that are appropriate given prior beliefs. So, for instance, if Mary judges that one *ought* to help those in need and she believes that John is in need (and she is in a position to help him), then it is appropriate for her to form a new belief, namely, that she *ought* to help John.

(*Ibid.*: 232, emphasis added)

So ought-commitments do seem, regarding their logical and grammatical trappings, to share the features that are characteristic of beliefs.

The third feature that suggests that ought-commitments are beliefs is what it is *like* to form an ought-commitment. Horgan and Timmons claim that our experience of ought-commitments is significantly similar to our experience of beliefs. In particular, we do not choose or infer what to believe in such cases. The same seems true of our ought-commitments. Say, for example, you attend a debate about human cloning. You have no view about whether cloning is right or wrong and sit and listen intently. Then one of the speakers says something and it strikes you that they are right that cloning is wrong. On reflection it did not feel as if you had reasoned to this view from another set of beliefs, but rather your experience is of *involuntarily* adopting it psychologically. It seems that this is the same as our experience of non-moral beliefs. For example, Horgan and Timmons list other experiential features that they think are also similar between beliefs and ought-commitments, not just the *involuntary* element.

If we grant, for the sake of argument, that there *are* significant grammatical, logical and experiential similarities between ought-commitments and beliefs, then Horgan and Timmons have evidence for the claim that ought-commitments are beliefs. "All of these features that are typical of ordinary belief – their grammatical and logical trappings … their experiential aspect – strongly suggest that ought-commitments are indeed genuine beliefs" (*ibid.*: 232–3).

This is how Horgan and Timmons set about the first task of showing the attraction of moral cognitivism; but what about the second task? What is stopping them from going all the way and claiming that moral beliefs are also descriptive? The answer is that they claim that there is a feature of moral judgement that strongly suggests that moral judgements are not descriptive.

Ought-commitments as non-descriptive

As we discussed in Chapter 9, moral judgements connect closely to motivation. For example, if I judge that it is wrong to pocket some money I find, then that is enough to motivate me not to do so. But on the other hand *descriptions* seem inert and unable in themselves to motivate us. It seems that it is only with some extra input perhaps from desires, hopes or wants that we can be motivated by a description. For Horgan and Timmons this is a good reason to think that moral beliefs are not descriptions.

> Typically ... moral judgements dispose one towards appropriate action in an especially direct way, independently of one's pre-existing desires and aversions. By contrast non-moral *descriptive* beliefs only become action-orientated in combination with prior desires or aversions.
>
> (*Ibid.*: 233, emphasis added)

If all this is right then Horgan and Timmons seem to have shown that there is good reason to be cognitivist but non-descriptivist. But why have other metaethicists not seen this – although Blackburn (e.g. 1998) has actually made similar moves – and also separated descriptions from belief? One reason is that the characteristics we associate with beliefs seem to be best explained in virtue of their being *descriptions*. This means that the evidence we give for cognitivism would also seem to count in favour of descriptivism. One such feature is the fact that moral judgements can apparently be true or false, so one reason to accept cognitivism is that it explains how the moral judgement that killing is wrong could be true or false. And beliefs must be *descriptive*, because one very natural way of explaining *how* judgements can be truth-apt is that they *are* descriptions. If a belief is true, then this is because it describes the world accurately; if it is false, then this is because the world does not meet the description.

So it seems that there is a choice for non-descriptive cognitivists: they can either make the strongest possible case for cognitivism by citing evidence from moral practice, but in so doing open up the possibility that some of the evidence relies on beliefs being descriptions; or, they can carefully show how some of the evidence for cognitivism does not rely on beliefs being descriptions and in so doing potentially weaken the justification for cognitivism by reducing the set of evidence.

Horgan and Timmons are well aware of these sorts of issues and develop an account of truth-aptness that does not rely on beliefs being descriptive. However overall we shall have to decide how closely the characteristics of beliefs they identify are themselves reliant on beliefs being descriptive. What is clear, though, is that Horgan and Timmons have highlighted an assumption running through metaethics that, when identified, could open up new areas of investigation and development.

Conclusion

We started this chapter by considering two fictionalist accounts: the hermeneutic fictionalist claims that we are currently involved in a moral fiction while the revolutionary fictionalist claims that we ought to engage in a moral fiction.

These accounts are attractive because they offer us a way of holding on to those features of our moral practice that suggest realism is correct, and rejecting realism, but not having to adopt error theory. They do this by not requiring there to be moral properties and facts in order for moral claims to be true. The fictionalist would claim that "giving to charity is right" could be true within the fiction, but not "literally true"; by doing so he does not need to answer awkward questions about the *property* of rightness.

The hermeneutic fictionalist has to give us a good reason to interpret our current moral practice as a fiction. One concern is whether this would be possible given that we do not recognize ourselves as being involved in moral make-believe. The revolutionary fictionalist has to give good reasons for a revolution. She might claim that given the truth of error theory it is of more practical benefit to engage in a fiction about morality than to abandon morality altogether. But we worried that a fictionalist account might not be able to give a strong enough reason to adopt fictionalism over eliminativism.

We finished this chapter with a discussion of Horgan and Timmons's account, which claims that moral judgements are expressions of belief, but a special type of *non-descriptive* belief. This account, like fictionalism, enjoys the benefits of cognitivism while avoiding error theory and side-stepping awkward questions about moral facts and properties.

Overall, what this chapter starts to show is that it is far from obvious how to distinguish even the most central claims in metaethics, such as cognitivism and non-cognitivism. It seems that we need new ways to conceptualize the metaethical terrain. Indeed some other positions such as ecumenical expressivism (e.g. Ridge 2006), realist non-cognitivism (e.g. Copp 2001) and cognitive irrealism (e.g. Skorupski 1999) are challenging some of the central ideas within metaethics.

THINGS TO REMEMBER

- Hermeneutic fictionalists are *not* error theorists.
- There is a difference between belief and make-believe.
- Both types of fictionalist can show that moral judgements can be true and false.
- Hermeneutic fictionalists argue that we may be engaged in a fiction, even though we do not recognize this.
- The revolutionary fictionalist does not think that we make-believe as a reaction to moral issues. Instead, we commit ourselves to make-believe so that we are already pretending when presented with moral issues.

Further reading

A good accessible discussion of fictionalism is Joyce (2005). A harder, but rewarding paper discussing fictionalism is Restall *et al.* (2005). A good general survey is Eklund (2009). The best introduction to Horgan and Timmons's view is Horgan & Timmons (2006); for a good but tough criticism of Horgan and Timmons's view see Barker (2002); for an excellent critique and discussion see Majors (2008). For some different but tough approaches to the metaethical debate see Skorupksi (1999), Copp (2001) and Ridge (2006).

Questions

Introduction

1. What is metaethics and how does it differ from applied and normative ethics?
2. What questions are metaethicists interested in?
3. Do you think that some metaethical questions are more important than others? If so, which?
4. When developing a metaethical theory, how much influence should be given to the way ordinary people think and talk?
5. Do you think that metaethics can have an impact on normative or applied ethics?
6. What, if any, might be the benefits of studying metaethics?

1. The open question argument

1. Can we define "good"?
2. What would be your definition of "good"?
3. What is the naturalistic fallacy, and how does it relate to the open question argument?
4. What is the difference between analytic and synthetic definitions?
5. Does claiming that something is good always motivate us?
6. Could the open question argument be used in areas other than ethics?

2. Emotivism

1. What is the relationship between science and philosophy?
2. What is the verification principle?

3. What is the difference between cognitivism and non-cognitivism?
4. Are there any genuine moral disagreements?
5. What are the advantages and disadvantages of emotivism?
6. What is the difference between emotivism, subjectivism and relativism?
7. Does the idea of a *moral* feeling make sense?
8. Can you be an emotivist in other areas, such as art or music? If so, what might such an account look like?

3. Error theory

1. Why might someone accept cognitivism?
2. Do you think that two people could agree on all the facts and reason correctly, but still have different moral views?
3. Why does Mackie think that if moral values existed they would be queer?
4. Is McDowell right in saying that something can be real but still mind-dependent?
5. If all our moral claims are false, why be moral?
6. Could it be useful to be an error theorist in other areas such as mathematics, aesthetics or theology?

4. Moral realism and naturalism

1. Why might someone be attracted to realism?
2. Do you think that people from different cultures might converge in their moral judgements?
3. Is there moral progress? Can you give some examples?
4. How might we test whether something is real?
5. What is the difference between the realist positions of Jackson, Railton and the Cornell realists?
6. If realism is right, will we find moral properties as part of the *natural* world?

5. Moral realism and non-naturalism

1. How would you characterize non-naturalism?
2. Why might someone adopt non-natural moral realism?
3. What do you understand by the term "normativity"?
4. Are some things, such as genocide, *always* wrong?
5. What is supervenience?
6. Is there a property or set of properties that all moral acts have in common?
7. Why might someone think there is a difference between constitution and identity?

8. What do you think of Shafer-Landau's argument, which draws on the nature of philosophy to make conclusions about ethics?

6. Quasi-realism

1. What are asserted and unasserted contexts? Can you give some examples?
2. What is the Frege–Geach problem?
3. What is quasi-realism? How does it differ from emotivism (Chapter 2)?
4. What is a "sensibility"? Why does Blackburn think this helps solve the Frege–Geach problem?
5. What is supervenience? Why might it cause a problem for realists?
6. What is minimalism about truth-aptness?

7. Moral relativism

1. What is the difference between speaker and agent relativism?
2. How far do you think someone's mental capacities affects whether his action is right or wrong?
3. What is the difference between normative and motivating reasons?
4. What is the difference between internal and external reasons?
5. Why might the speaker relativist have a problem dealing with moral disagreements?
6. Could we be speaker relativists in other areas, such as religion or mathematics?

8. Moral psychology

1. Do you think a psychopath can make genuine moral judgements?
2. What is internalism?
3. What is externalism?
4. What is Michael Smith's attack on externalism and does it succeed?
5. Do you think that moral beliefs could motivate in the absence of desires?
6. What is Michael Smith's moral problem?

9. Moral epistemology

1. Can we have moral knowledge?
2. What is the epistemic regress argument?
3. What is intuitionism?
4. What is coherentism?
5. Is intuitionism or coherentism more plausible?

6. How might the issues in moral epistemology influence other areas of meta-ethics – in particular, issues to do with realism?

10. Fictionalism and non-descriptive cognitivism

1. What is revolutionary fictionalism?
2. What is hermeneutic fictionalism?
3. What would the world be like without morality? Would you like to live in such a world?
4. Why do Horgan and Timmons think that our moral judgements express non-descriptive beliefs?
5. Does a *non-descriptive* belief makes sense?
6. What are the advantages and disadvantages of cognitive non-descriptivism?

Glossary

agent relativism   The agent relativist argues that someone's action is right or wrong depending on his or her moral framework.

amoralist   An agent who is psychologically normal but who is unmotivated by her moral judgements. The externalist about motivation thinks amoralists are common. The internalist about motivation thinks that the amoralist is a *conceptual impossibility*.

anti-realism   *see* **non-realism**

analytic definition   A definition whose truth can be established via conceptual analysis.

analytic naturalism   The view that we can define central moral terms as non-moral, natural ones. This may be done via conceptual analysis.

analytic truth   A claim is analytically true if its truth relies solely on the meaning of terms involved, for example, "A bachelor is an unmarried man".

a posteriori   We know something *a posteriori* if we know it through experience.

a priori   We know something *a priori* if we know it independent of experience, for example, knowledge of mathematical and logical truths.

closed question   A question is "closed" if the meanings of the terms in the question decide the matter, for example, "Matt is a bachelor, but is he married?"

cognitivism   The view that moral judgements express beliefs which describe some sector of reality. It is a consequence of this that moral judgements are **truth-apt**.

cognitive non-descriptivism   Sometimes called "non-descriptive cognitivism" or "cognitive expressivism", it is the view that moral judgements express beliefs but that these beliefs are non-descriptive.

conceptual analysis   The breaking down of concepts into their constitutive parts.

For example, the conceptual analysis of "square" would be "a plane rectangle with four equal sides and four right angles".

Cornell realism The view that moral properties exist and are irreducible (*sui generis*), natural properties.

correspondence theory of truth The view that there is a property of truth that some suitably structured utterances have, and that such things get to be true because they correspond with the world.

coherence account of knowledge The idea that a belief is justified if it is part of the most coherent set of beliefs. Coherentism accepts *holistic justification* and rejects *linear justification*.

counterfactual test A test for explanatory relevance. To say that *a*'s being *F* is explanatorily relevant to *b*'s being *G* is to say that if *a* had not been *F* then *b* would not have been *G* (Miller 2003: 145).

"direction of fit" metaphor A metaphorical way of distinguishing between belief and desire. Beliefs are said to "change to fit the world"; desires are said to "change the world to fit them".

divine command theory The view that someone is morally right if and only if God commands it. Something is wrong if and only if God forbids it.

emotivism A form of **non-cognitivism** that holds that moral judgements are expressions of the speaker's emotions rather than a description of anything. This is not to be confused with **subjectivism** or **relativism**.

error theory Error theorists are cognitivists but not realists. They argue that moral judgements describe the world as having objective value, but that the world does not contain any objective value. Consequently all moral judgements are systematically and uniformly false.

externalism about motivation The view that the link between moral judgement and motivation is *contingent*. An agent is motivated to do what they judge to be right if he has the right desire – normally described as the *desire to do what is right*.

external reasons The view that if an agent has moral reason to act, then the grounding for such a reason can be based on things other than the desires, commitments, beliefs and general projects that are important to the agent.

Frege–Geach problem Supposedly *the* challenge for non-cognitivists. It shows that non-cognitivists are committed to the counter-intuitive and problematic view that the meaning of moral terms varies across asserted and unasserted contexts.

hermeneutic fictionalism Hermeneutic fictionalists argue that even though most people never recognize it, there are good reasons to think that our moral practice is based on make-believe and that we are involved in a moral fiction.

Humean theory of motivation The view that motivation only arises when a belief combines with an appropriately related desire – where desire takes the lead role.

Further it is the view that beliefs and desires are distinct mental states such that a belief cannot entail a desire.

internalism about motivation   The view that there is a conceptual and necessary connection between moral judgement and motivation. For example, if an agent judges it is right to give money to charity then as a matter of conceptual necessity they will be motivated to give money to charity.

internalism about motivation (weak)   The view that there is a necessary but defeasible connection between moral judgement and motivation. For example, if an agent judges it is right to give money to charity – and they are not suffering any weakness of will and the like – then as a matter of conceptual necessity they will be motivated to give money to charity.

internal reasons   The view (roughly) that if agent has moral reason to act, then the grounding for such a reason is based on the desires, commitments, beliefs and general projects that are important to the agent.

intuitionism   A view in moral epistemology that holds that there is at least one moral belief, and possibly many, that are self-evidently justifiable. This does not rule out other ways of justifying moral claims, nor does it mean that intuitionists believe judges to be infallible.

irrealism   *see* **non-realism**

minimalism about truth   The most popular alternative account of truth among non-cognitivists. Such an account is minimal because according to it a claim could be true, even though there is no fact that makes it so. Strictly speaking, for the minimalist the answer to "What makes moral claims true?" is "Nothing". For the minimalist about truth, "Murder is wrong is true" just means murder is wrong, and asking whether murder is wrong is just to ask whether we should accept that murder is wrong.

minimalism about truth-aptitude   The view that if the central claims of a practice seem truth-apt, then they are. In particular, the language would have to be disciplined (there are acknowledged standards for the proper and improper use) and the language would have to have the right sort of syntactic features (e.g. it can be embedded, negated, conjoined, etc.).

moral problem   Michael Smith's (1994) name for the tension between three apparently intuitive positions: **internalism about motivation**, the **Humean account of motivation** and **cognitivism**.

motivating reason   The reasons that motivate people to act: for example, that I want to go for a swim is a motivating reason for me to jump into the spring.

naturalistic fallacy   G. E. Moore's name for the attempt to reduce the property good.

naturalism   The naturalist claims that the only things that exist are those that would appear in the scientific picture of what exists.

non-cognitivism   The view that moral judgements express non-cognitive states such as desires, emotions, prescriptions and norms of acceptance. Consequently, for the non-cognitivist moral judgments are often thought not to be **truth-apt**.

non-naturalist The non-naturalist thinks that there are some things that exist which could not show up on the scientific picture of what exists.

normative reason A reason someone has to act in certain ways that do not seem obviously linked to their psychological states. You have a reason not to swim in the spring because it is 110 degrees, even though you may want to swim.

open question argument G. E. Moore's method for identifying and demonstrating instances of the **naturalistic fallacy**.

open questions A question is open if the meanings of the terms in the question do not decide the matter. For example, "Is darts a sport?"

paradox of analysis The claim that there are convincing reasons to think that conceptual analyses can be informative and unobvious but also convincing reasons to think that conceptual analyses cannot be informative and unobvious.

proposition The non-linguistic entity expressed by a sentence. Two sentences which express the same proposition have the same meaning, despite the fact that they may say different things: for example, "I am happy" and "Je suis heureux" express the same proposition.

quasi-realism The ongoing explanatory programme that attempts to show how by starting from **non-realism** we can mimic the features supposedly definitive of **realism**.

realism The moral realist argues that moral properties and/or facts exist and are in some way independent from people's judgements.

reductionism Refers to either ontological or semantic reduction. Semantic reductionism is the conceptual analysis of moral terms in non-moral ones. Ontological reductionism is the claim that moral properties are non-moral, natural properties.

relativism *see* **agent relativism** and **speaker relativism**

revolutionary fictionalism The view that the appropriate response to our current moral practice is to treat morality as a fiction. This is typically adopted as a response to **error theory**, although it need not be.

scepticism The view that we are not justified in our moral beliefs and consequently do not have moral knowledge.

speaker relativism According to speaker relativism, when we make a moral judgement what we are saying is elliptical and can only be judged as true or false in relation to my moral framework.

subjectivism The view that when we make a moral judgement we are describing our own mental states, such as approval and disapproval. When I say "Killing is wrong" I am telling you that I have a certain attitude towards killing. Because subjectivism thinks moral judgements express beliefs (about the speaker's mental states) it is a *cognitivist* theory. It should *not* be confused with **non-cognitivism** or **emotivism**.

sui generis   Literally, "of its own kind". *Sui generis* properties are irreducible. For example, Cornell realists think that moral properties are *sui generis*.

supervenience   The view that two situations cannot be different in their moral properties without differing in their natural properties. We are meant to know this *a priori*.

synthetic definition   A definition whose truth cannot be established via conceptual analysis alone, for example "Water is H_2O".

synthetic truth   A claim is synthetically true if it does not rely solely on the meaning of terms involved, for example, if true, "It is raining".

truth-apt   A judgement is truth-apt if it is capable of being true or false. The judgement that it is raining is truth-apt, whereas the exclamation "Ow!" is not.

truth-maker thesis   A claim is true if and only if some feature of the world, such as properties, makes it true.

unasserted claim   A claim is unasserted when it is used but not asserted, for example "If the world flooded then I would need to swim"; "the world flooded" is mentioned but not asserted. There are many ways we can mention but not assert claims, for example if they appear in "... and ...", "... or ..." or "if ... then ..." questions and reports.

verification principle   The principle that states that if a sentence is not analytic or potentially empirically verifiable then it is meaningless.

References

Adams, R. 1979. "Divine Command Metaethics Modified Again". *Journal of Religious Ethics* **7**(1): 66–79.

Alexander, J. & J. Weinberg 2007. "Analytic Epistemology and Experimental Philosophy". *Philosophy Compass* **2**(1): 56–80.

Altman, A. 2004. "Breathing Life into a Dead Argument: G. E. Moore and the Open Question Argument". *Philosophical Studies* **117**(3): 395–408.

Arenella, P. 1990. "Character, Choice and Moral Agency: The Relevance of Character to Our Moral Culpability Judgments". *Social Philosophy and Policy* **7**(2): 59–83.

Armstrong, D. 2004. *Truth and Truthmakers*. Cambridge: Cambridge University Press.

Audi, R. 1998. "Moderate Intuitionism and the Epistemology of Moral Judgment". *Ethical Theory and Moral Practice* **1**(1): 15–44.

Ayer, A. J. 1959. *Logical Positivism*. Glencoe, IL: Free Press.

Ayer, A. J. [1936] 1974. *Language, Truth and Logic*. Harmondsworth: Penguin.

Baldwin, T. 1990. *G. E. Moore*. London: Routledge.

Ball, S. 1991. "Linguistic Intuitions and Varieties of Ethical Naturalism". *Philosophy and Phenomenological Research* **51**(1): 1–38.

Barker, S. 2002. "Troubles with Horgan and Timmons' Nondescriptive Cognitivism". *Grazer Philosophische Studien* **63**: 235–55.

BBC 2007. "Pole Wakes Up from 19-year Coma". http://news.bbc.co.uk/1/hi/6715313.stm (accessed May 2011).

Bird, A. & E. Tobin 2008. "Natural Kinds". *Stanford Encyclopedia of Philosophy*. http://plato.stanford.edu/entries/natural-kinds/ (accessed April 2011).

Blackburn, S. 1984. *Spreading the Word*. Oxford: Oxford University Press.

Blackburn, S. 1993. *Essays in Quasi-Realism*. New York: Oxford University Press.

Blackburn, S. 1998. *Ruling Passions*. Oxford: Oxford University Press.

Blackburn, S. 2000. "Relativism". In *The Blackwell Guide to Ethical Theory*, H. LaFollette (ed.), 38–52. Oxford: Blackwell.

Blackburn, S. 2005. "Quasi-Realism no Fictionalism". In *Fictionalism in Metaphysics*, M. E. Kalderon (ed.), 322–38. Oxford: Oxford University Press.

Blackburn, S. 2007. "How to be an Ethical Anti-Realist". In *Foundations of Ethics: An Anthology*, R. Shafer-Landau & T. Cuneo (eds), 47–58. Oxford: Blackwell.

Boghossian, P. 2006a. *Fear of Knowledge: Against Relativism and Constructivism*. New York: Oxford University Press.

Boghossian, P. 2006b. "What is Relativism?" In *Truth and Realism*, P. Greenough & M. P. Lynch (eds), 13–37. Oxford: Oxford University Press.

Bonjour, L. 1988. *The Structure of Empirical Knowledge*. Cambridge, MA: Harvard University Press.

Boyd, R. 1988. "How to be a Moral Realist". In *Essays on Moral Realism*, G. Sayre-McCord (ed.), 181–228. Ithaca, NY: Cornell University Press.

Braddon-Mitchell, D. & R. Nola (eds) 2009. *Conceptual Analysis and Philosophical Naturalism*. Cambridge, MA: MIT Press.

Brink, D. 1984. "Moral Realism and the Sceptical Arguments from Disagreement and Queerness". *Australasian Journal of Philosophy* 62(2): 111–25.

Chappell, T. 2008. "Moral Perception". *Philosophy* 83(4): 421–37.

Clark, M. 2002. *Paradoxes from A to Z*. London: Routledge.

Cleckley, H. 1941. *The Mask of Sanity: An Attempt to Reinterpret the So-called Psychopathic Personality*. St Louis, MO: C. V. Mosby Company.

Copp, D. 2001. "Realist-Expressivism: A Neglected Option for Moral Realism". *Social Philosophy and Policy* 18(2): 1–43.

Copp, D. 2003. "Why Naturalism?" *Ethical Theory and Moral Practice* 6(2): 179–200.

Copp, D. 2005. *The Oxford Handbook of Ethical Theory*. New York: Oxford University Press.

Cullison, A. 2010. "Moral Perception". *European Journal of Philosophy* 18(2): 159–75.

Cuneo, T. 2007. "Recent Faces of Moral Nonnaturalism". *Philosophy Compass* 2: 850–79.

Cushman, F. 2010. "Don't be Afraid – Science Can Make us Better". *New Scientist* 2782: 41–3.

Daly, C. & D. Liggins 2010. "In Defence of Error Theory". *Philosophical Studies* 149(2): 209–30.

Dancy, J. 1993. *Moral Reasons*. Oxford: Blackwell.

Darwall, S., A. Gibbard & P. Railton 1992. "Toward Fin de siècle Ethics: Some Trends". *The Philosophical Review* 101(1): 115–89.

Descartes, R. [1641] 1996. *Meditations on First Philosophy*. Cambridge: Cambridge University Press.

Eklund, M. 2009. "Fictionalism". *Stanford Encyclopedia of Philosophy*. http://plato.stanford.edu/entries/fictionalism/ (accessed April 2011).

Engel, P. 2002. *Truth*. Chesham: Acumen.

Finlay, S. 2007. "Four Faces of Moral Realism". *Philosophy Compass* 2(6): 820–49.

Finlay, S. 2008. "The Error in the Error Theory". *Australasian Journal of Philosophy* 86(3): 347–69.

Finlay, S. 2010. "Recent Work on Normativity". *Analysis* 70(2): 331–46.

Fisher, A. & S. Kirchin (eds) 2006. *Arguing about Metaethics*. Abingdon: Routledge.

FitzPatrick, W. 2009. "Recent Work on Ethical Realism". *Analysis* 69(4): 746–60.

Francén, R. 2009. "No Deep Disagreement for New Relativists". *Philosophical Studies* 151(1): 19–37.

Frankena, W. K. 1939. "The Naturalistic Fallacy". *Mind* **48**(192): 464–77.

Garner, R. 1990. "On the Genuine Queerness of Moral Properties and Facts". *Australasian Journal of Philosophy* **68**(2): 137–46.

Garner, R. 2007. "Abolishing Morality". *Ethical Theory and Moral Practice* **10**(5): 499–513.

Geach, P. 1958. "Imperative and Deontic Logic". *Analysis* **18**(3): 49–56.

Geach, P. 1960. "Ascriptivism". *Philosophical Review* **69**: 221–5.

Geach, P. 1965. "Assertion". *Philosophical Review* **65**: 449–65.

Gibbard, A. 1990. *Wise Choices, Apt Feelings*. Oxford: Clarendon Press.

Gibbard, A. 2003. *Thinking How to Live*. Cambridge, MA: Harvard University Press.

Guerrero, A. 2007. "Don't Know, Don't Kill: Moral Ignorance Culpability and Caution". *Philosophical Studies* **136**(1): 59–97.

Haddon, M. 2004. *The Curious Incident of the Dog in the Night-Time*. London: Vintage.

Haji, I. 1998. "On Psychopaths and Culpability". *Law and Philosophy* **17**(2): 117–40.

Haldane, J. 1928. *Possible Worlds and Other Papers*. London: Chatto & Windus.

Hales, S. 2011. *A Companion to Relativism*. Oxford: Wiley-Blackwell.

Hare, R. M. 1952. *The Language of Morals*. Oxford: Oxford University Press.

Hargreaves, R. 1981. *Little Miss Shy*. Manchester: Egmont Publishing.

Harman, G. 1977. *The Nature of Morality*. Oxford: Oxford University Press.

Harman, G. 2000. *Explaining Value: And Other Essays in Moral Philosophy*. Oxford: Oxford University Press.

Harman, G. & J. Thomson 1996. *Moral Relativism and Moral Objectivity*. Oxford: Blackwell.

Horgan, T. & M. Timmons 1992. "Troubles for New Wave Moral Semantics: The 'Open Question Argument' Revived". *Philosophical Papers* **21**: 153–75.

Horgan, T. & M. Timmons 2000. "Nondescriptivist Cognitivism: Framework for a New Metaethic". *Philosophical Papers* **29**(2): 121–53.

Horgan, T. & M. Timmons 2006. "Morality without Facts". In *Contemporary Debates in Moral Theory*, J. Dreier (ed.), 220–40. Oxford: Blackwell.

Humberstone, I. L. 1992. "Direction of Fit". *Mind* **101**(401): 59–84.

Hume, D. [1748] 1995. *An Enquiry Concerning Human Understanding*. Oxford: Oxford University Press.

Jackson, F. 1982. "Epiphenomenal Qualia". *Philosophical Quarterly* **32**: 127–36.

Jackson, F. 1998. *From Metaphysics to Ethics*. Oxford: Oxford University Press.

Jackson, F., K. Mason & S. Stich 2009. "Folk Psychology and Tacit Theories: A Correspondence between Frank Jackson, and Steve Stich and Kelby Mason". In *Conceptual Analysis and Philosophical Naturalism*, D. Braddon-Mitchell & R. Nola (eds), 45–98. Cambridge, MA: MIT Press.

Jacobs, J. 2002. *Dimensions of Moral Theory: An Introduction to Metaethics and Moral Psychology*. Oxford: Blackwell.

Joyce, R. 2001. *The Myth of Morality*. Cambridge: Cambridge University Press.

Joyce, R. 2002. "Theistic Ethics and the Euthyphro Dilemma". *Journal of Religous Ethics* **30**(1): 49–75.

Joyce, R. 2005. "Moral Fictionalism". In *Fictionalism in Metaphysics*, M. Kalderon (ed.), 287–313. Oxford: Oxford University Press.

Joyce, R. forthcoming. "Error-Theory". In *International Encylopedia of Ethics*, H. LaFollette (ed.). Oxford: Wiley-Blackwell.

Joyce, R. & S. Kirchin (eds) 2010. *A World without Values: Essays on John Mackie's Moral Error Theory*. Dordrecht: Springer.

Korsgaard, C. 1996. *The Sources of Normativity*. Cambridge: Cambridge University Press.

LaFollette, H. 2000. *The Blackwell Guide to Ethical Theory*. Oxford: Blackwell.

Leiter, B. 2001. "Moral Facts and Best Explanations". *Social Philosophy and Policy* **18**: 79–101.

Lenman, J. 2006. "Moral Naturalism". *Stanford Encyclopedia of Philosophy*. http://plato.stanford.edu/entries/naturalism-moral/ (accessed April 2011).

Levy, N. 2002. *Moral Relativism: A Short Introduction*. Oxford: Oneworld.

Lewis, D. 1970. "How to Define Theoretical Terms". *Journal of Philosophy* **67**: 427–46.

Lewis, D. 1972. "General Semantics". In *Semantics of Natural Language*, D. Davidson & G. Harman (eds), 169–218. Dordrecht: D. Reidel.

Lillehammer, H. 1997. "Smith on Moral Fetishism". *Analysis* **57**(3): 187–95.

Lillehammer, H. 2000. "The Doctrine of Internal Reasons". *Journal of Value Inquiry* **34**: 507–16.

Locke, J. [1690] 1975. *An Essay Concerning Human Understanding*, P. H. Nidditch (ed.). Oxford: Clarendon.

Lowe, E. J. 2000. *An Introduction to the Philosophy of Mind*. Cambridge: Cambridge University Press.

Mabrito, R. 2005. "Does Shafer-Landau Have a Problem with Supervenience?" *Philosophical Studies* **126**(2): 297–311.

MacFarlane, J. 2007. "Relativism and Disagreement". *Philosophical Studies* **132**: 17–31.

Mackie, J. 1977. *Ethics: Inventing Right and Wrong*. New York: Penguin.

Majors, B. 2007. "Moral Explanation". *Philosophy Compass* **2**(1): 1–15.

Majors, B. 2008. "Cognitivist Expressivism and the Nature of Belief". *Ethical Theory and Moral Practice* **11**(3): 279–93.

McDermott, T. 1993. *Aquinas: Selected Writings*. Oxford: Oxford University Press.

McDowell, J. 1985. "Values and Secondary Qualities". In *Morality and Objectivity*, T. Honderich (ed.), 110–29. London: Routledge.

McDowell, J. 1987. *Projection and Truth in Ethics*. Lindley Lecture 1987. Department of Philosophy, University of Kansas.

McDowell, J. 1998. *Mind, Value, and Reality*. Cambridge, MA: Harvard University Press.

McNaughton, D. (1988). *Moral Vision*. Oxford: Blackwell.

Miller, A. 1996. "An Objection to Smith's Argument from Externalism". *Analysis* **56**(3): 169–74.

Miller, A. 1998. "Emotivism and the Verification Principle". *Proceedings of the Aristotelian Society* **98**: 103–24.

Miller, A. 2003. *An Introduction to Contemporary Metaethics*. Oxford: Polity.

Miller, A. 2007. *Philosophy of Language*. Abingdon: Routledge.

Miller, A. 2010. "Realism". *Stanford Encyclopedia of Philosophy*. http://plato.stanford.edu/entries/realism/ (accessed April 2011).

Millgram, E. 1995. "Was Hume a Humean?" *Hume Studies* **31**(1): 75–93.

Millgram, E. 1996. "Williams' Argument against External Reasons". *Noûs* **30**: 197–220.

Moore, G. E. 1939. "Proof of an External World". *Proceedings of the British Academy* **25**: 273–300.

Moore, G. E. [1903] 1993. *Principia Ethica*. Cambridge: Cambridge University Press.

Mulligan, K. & F. Correia 2008. "Facts". *Stanford Encylopedia of Philosophy*. http://plato.stanford.edu/entries/facts/ (accessed April 2011).

Murdoch, I. 1970. *The Sovereignty of Good*. London: Routledge.

Murphy, M. 2008. "Theological Voluntarism". *Stanford Encyclopedia of Philosophy*. http://plato.stanford.edu/entries/voluntarism-theological/ (accessed April 2011).

O'Brien, D. 2006. *An Introduction to the Theory of Knowledge*. Cambridge: Polity.

Plantinga, A. 1998. "Afterword". In *The Analytic Theist: an Alvin Plantinga Reader*, J. Sennett (ed.), 353–9. Cambridge MA: Eerdmans.

Plato 1981. *Euthyphro*. In Plato, *Five Dialogues*, G. M. A. Grube (trans.). Indianapolis, IN: Hackett.

Plato 2003. *The Republic*, D. Lee (trans.). London: Penguin.

Quinn, P. L. 1978. *Divine Commands and Moral Requirements*. Oxford: Oxford University Press.

Quinn, P. L. 2000. "Divine Command Theory". In *The Blackwell Guide to Ethical Theory*, H. LaFollette (ed.), 53–73. Oxford: Blackwell.

Rachels, J. 2000. "Naturalism". In *The Blackwell Guide to Ethical Theory*, H. LaFollette (ed.), 74–91. Oxford: Blackwell.

Railton, P. 1986. "Moral Realism". *Philosophical Review* **95**(2): 163–207.

Railton, P. 2003. *Facts, Values, and Norms: Essays toward a Morality of Consequence*. Cambridge: Cambridge University Press.

Restall, G., with D. Nolan & C. West 2005. "Moral Fictionalism versus The Rest". *Australasian Journal of Philosophy* **83**: 307–29.

Ridge, M. 2006. "Ecumenical Expressivism: The Best of Both Worlds?" In *Oxford Studies in Metaethics*, vol. 2, R. Shafer-Landau (ed.), 302–36. Oxford: Oxford University Press.

Ridge, M. 2007. "Anti-Reductionism and Supervenience". *Journal of Moral Philosophy* **4**(3): 330–48.

Ridge, M. & S. McKeever 2008. "Preempting Principle: Recent Debates in Moral Particularism". *Philosophy Compass* **3**(6): 177–92.

Rogers, B. 2000. *A. J. Ayer: A Life*. London: Vintage.

Rosati, C. 1995. "Naturalism, Normativity, and the Open Question Argument". *Noûs* **29**(1): 46–70.

Rosen, G. 1998. "Essays in Quasi-Realism by Simon Blackburn". *Noûs* **32**(3): 386–405.

Rosen, G. 2003. "Culpability and Ignorance". *Proceedings of the Aristotelian Society* **103**(1): 61–84.

Roskies, A. 2003. "Are Ethical Judgments Intrinsically Motivational? Lessons From 'Acquired Sociopathy'". *Philosophical Psychology* **16**(1): 51–66.

Ross, W. D. 1930. *The Right and the Good*. Oxford: Clarendon Press.

Russell, B. [1922] 1999. "Is There an Absolute Good?" In *Russell on Ethics*, C. Pidgen (ed.), 119–25. New York: Routledge.

Sadler, B. 2003. "The Possibility of Amoralism: A Defence Against Internalism". *Philosophy* **78**(303): 63–78.

Sanford, D. 1984. "Infinite Regress Arguments". In *Principles of Philosophical Reasoning*, J. S. Fetzer & G. Schlesinger (eds), 94–117. Totowa, NJ: Rowman & Littlefield.

Sayre-McCord, G. 1986. "The Many Moral Realisms". *Southern Journal of Philosophy* **24**: 1–22.

Sayre-McCord, G. 1988. *Essays on Moral Realism*. Ithaca, NY: Cornell University Press.

Sayre-McCord, G. 1996. "Coherentist Epistemology and Moral Theory". In *Moral Knowledge?*, W. Sinnott-Armstrong & M. Timmons (eds), 137–89. Oxford: Oxford University Press.

Schilpp, P. 1952. *The Philosophy of G. E. Moore*. New York: Tudor Publishing.

Schroeder, M. 2008. "What is the Frege–Geach Problem?" *Philosophy Compass* **3**(4): 703–20.

Schroeder, M. 2010. *Non-Cognitivism in Ethics*. Abingdon: Routledge.

Searle, J. 1962. "Meaning and Speech Acts". *Philosophical Review* **71**: 423–32.

Shafer-Landau, R. 2003. *Moral Realism: A Defence*. Oxford: Oxford University Press.

Shafer-Landau, R. 2007a. *Ethical Theory: An Anthology*. Oxford: Blackwell.

Shafer-Landau, R. 2007b. "Ethics as Philosophy: A Defense of Ethical Nonnaturalism". In *Foundations of Ethics*, R. Shafer-Landau & T. Cuneo (eds), 62–72. Oxford: Blackwell.

Shafer-Landau, R. 2007c. "Moral and Theological Realism: The Explanatory Argument". *Journal of Moral Philosophy* **4**(3): 311–29.

Shaver, R. 2007. "Non-Naturalism". In *Themes from G. E. Moore: New Essays in Epistemology and Ethics*, S. S. Nuccetelli & G. Seay (eds), 283–307. New York: Oxford University Press.

Simpson, E. 1999. "Between Internalism and Externalism in Ethics". *Philosophical Quarterly* **49**(195): 201–14.

Sinclair, N. 2009. "Recent Work in Expressivism". *Analysis* **69**(1): 136–47.

Singer, P. 2007. "Should we Trust Our Moral Intuitions?". http://www.utilitarian. net/singer/by/200703-.htm (accessed April 2011).

Sinnott-Armstrong, W. 2006. *Moral Skepticisms*. New York: Oxford University Press.

Skorupski, J. 1999. "Irrealist Cognitivism". *Ratio* **12**: 436–59.

Skorupski, J. 2007. "Internal Reasons and the Scope of Blame". In *Bernard Williams*, A. Thomas (ed.), 73–103. Cambridge: Cambridge University Press.

Smith, M. 1994. *The Moral Problem*. Oxford: Blackwell.

Smith, M. 1996. "The Argument for Internalism: Reply to Miller". *Analysis* **56**(3): 175–83.

Snare, F. 1975. "The Open-Question as a Linguistic Test". *Ratio* **17**: 122–9.

Stanley, J. 2001. "Hermeneutic Fictionalism". *Midwest Studies in Philosophy* **25**(1): 36–71.

Stevenson, C. 1937. "The Emotive Meaning of Ethical Terms". *Mind* **46**(181): 14–31.

Stevenson, C. 1944. *Ethics and Language*. New Haven, CT: Yale University Press.

Strandberg, C. 2004. "In Defence of the Open Question Argument". *Journal of Ethics* **8**(2): 179–96.

Swain, S., J. Alexander & J. Weinberg 2008. "The Instability of Philosophical Intuitions: Running Hot and Cold on Truetemp". *Philosophy and Phenomenological Research* **76**(1): 138–55.

Swoyer, C. 2009. "Properties". *Stanford Encyclopedia of Philosophy.* http://plato.stanford.edu/entries/properties/ (accessed April 2011).

Tallant, J. 2011. *Metaphysics: An Introduction.* New York: Continuum.

Tersman, F. 2006. *Moral Disagreement.* New York: Cambridge University Press.

Timmons, M. 1999. *Morality without Foundation.* New York: Oxford University.

Totten, S., W. S. Parsons & I. W. Charny 2009. *Century of Genocide.* New York: Routledge.

Wierenga, E. 1983. "A Defensible Divine Command Theory". *Noûs* **17**(3): 387–407.

Williams, B. 1972. *Morality: An Introduction to Ethics.* Cambridge: Cambridge University Press.

Williams, B. 1981. *Moral Luck.* Cambridge: Cambridge University Press.

Williams, B. 1985. *Ethics and the Limits of Philosophy.* London: Fontana.

Wolfberg, P. J. 1999. *Play and Imagination in Children With Autism.* New York: Teachers College Press.

Wong, D. 2006. *Natural Moralities: A Defense of Pluralistic Relativism.* Oxford: Oxford University Press.

Wright, C. 1987. "Realism, Anti-Realism, Irrealism, Quasi-Realism". *Midwest Studies in Philosophy* **12**: 25–49.

Wright, C. 1989. "The Verification Principle: Another Puncture – Another Patch". *Mind* **98**(392): 611–22.

Wright, C. 1992. *Truth and Objectivity.* Cambridge, MA: Harvard University Press.

Zangwill, N. 2003. "Externalist Moral Motivation". *American Philosophical Quarterly* **40**(2): 143–54.

Zangwill, N. 2008. "Besires and the Motivation Debate". *Theoria* **74**(1): 50–59.

Index

Printed in the USA/Agawam, MA
July 17, 2015

619445.009